A HISTORY OF THE ISLE OF MAN

by

R. H. KINVIG, M.A.
Professor of Geography
University of Birmingham

PUBLISHED
UNDER THE AUSPICES OF TYNWALD
BY THE MANX MUSEUM
AND ANCIENT MONUMENTS TRUSTEES

UNIVERSITY PRESS OF LIVERPOOL
1950

TO

MY WIFE

FIRST EDITION . . . 1944
SECOND EDITION . . 1950

Printed in England by Eaton Press Ltd., Liverpool

PREFACE

The publication of a new edition of this History, first published at the end of 1944, has been made possible by the Trustees of the Manx Museum, who made a grant from funds provided by Tynwald for the purpose, and I am very grateful to all concerned for the assistance thus given. I have taken the opportunity of revising the text in the light, both of fresh discoveries that have been made, particularly in the archaeological field, and of the important political developments that have taken place in recent years. Some changes have also been made in the maps and other illustrations.

As noted in the first edition of this book many friends have helped in its production and I wish to thank them all for their advice and criticism. I especially wish to acknowledge the assistance of Mr. David Craine, M.A. in the preparation of the Glossary, which is a new feature, also the valuable guidance from Mr. J. D. Qualtrough, C.B.E., the Speaker of the House of Keys, Mr. Ramsey Moore, the former Attorney General, Mr. Neil Mathieson, of the Isle of Man Natural History and Antiquarian Society, Mr. W. F. Cringle of Government Office, Douglas, and Professor E. G. Bowen, of Aberystwyth. Finally, I am particularly grateful to Mr. B. R. S. Megaw, B.A., F.S.A., Director of the Manx Museum, and to Mr. R. A. Downie of the University Press of Liverpool, for help in many ways.

R. H. KINVIG

Department of Geography,
University of Birmingham.
February, 1950.

CONTENTS

ILLUSTRATIONS

ACKNOWLEDGMENTS

I am very grateful to *The Illustrated London News* for permission to reproduce *fig. 17*, and to *Picture Post* for *fig. 48*; also to the National Museum of Wales for the loan of the block for *fig. 28*, as well as to the Manx Museum and the Isle of Man Publicity Board for the use of many views and blocks. I am much indebted to Mr. D. W. Oliver who has drawn the Maps for *figs. 4, 5 and 14*.

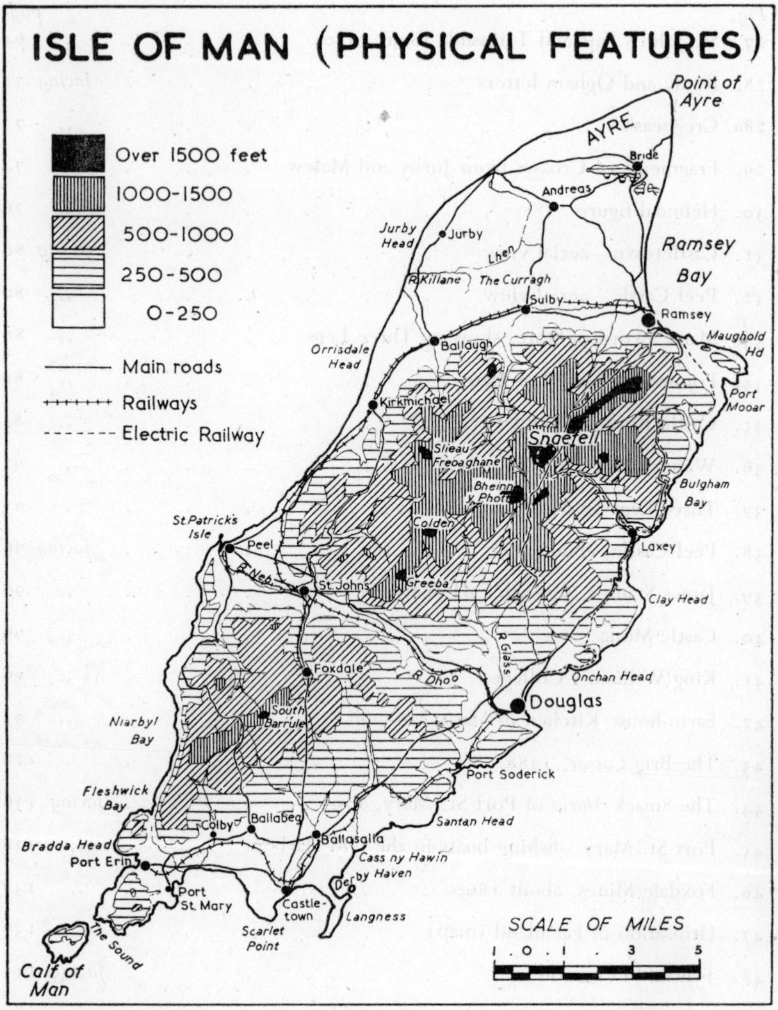
ISLE OF MAN (PHYSICAL FEATURES)
Over 1500 feet
1000-1500
500-1000
250-500
0-250
Main roads
Railways
Electric Railway
Point of Ayre
AYRE
Bride
Andreas
Jurby Head
Jurby
Lhen
Ramsey Bay
R. Killane
The Curragh
Sulby
Ramsey
Ballaugh
Orrisdale Head
Maughold Hd
Port Mooar
Kirkmichael
Snaefell
Slieau Freoaghane
Bheinn y Phott
Bulgham Bay
Colden
St. Patrick's Isle
Peel
Laxey
R. Neb
St. Johns
Greeba
Clay Head
R. Glass
Foxdale
R. Dhoo
Onchan Head
Douglas
Niarbyl Bay
South Barrule
Port Soderick
Fleshwick Bay
Santan Head
Colby
Ballabeg
Ballasalla
Bradda Head
Cass ny Hawin
Port Erin
Derby Haven
Port St. Mary
Castletown
Langness
Scarlet Point
The Sound
Calf of Man
SCALE OF MILES
1 0 1 3 5

Chapter I.

THE PHYSICAL AND HUMAN BACKGROUND

Position of the Island

Placed as it is in the middle of the Irish Sea, the Isle of Man has received many influences from neighbouring lands—England, Scotland, Ireland and Wales—from all of which it is often clearly visible. At the present day English influence is the most important as it has been for some centuries, but in some of the earlier periods of Manx history, Ireland, particularly northern Ireland, has played a very significant part; while south-west Scotland, which is nearest of all to the Island, has also been extremely important at various times, as, for example, during the early days of Christianity.

The Irish Sea opens southward through St. George's Channel and beyond Land's End to the shores of western France, Spain and Portugal; and there is no doubt that in very early times, before the days of written history, traders from the Mediterranean followed this route and brought ideas from that distant region to the Isle of Man as well as to the other lands surrounding it. There is another open sea passage through the North Channel to the Western Isles of Scotland, and on round the north of that country to Scandinavia; and by this route during the eighth and the following centuries A.D. came the Norse Vikings to conquer Man and to settle in it.

Many varied streams have therefore entered into the main current of Manx life, and the details will be examined in the following chapters of this book. But in the present chapter it will be helpful to think a little further not only about the general position of the Island in relation to the British Isles, but also about some important features concerning the nature of the land and its people in the past and at the present.

The Highland and Lowland Regions of Britain

Great Britain may be divided into two contrasted portions—a north-western and a south-eastern—by a line drawn broadly from the mouth of the Tees round the southern end of the Pennines, and thence south-west to the neighbourhood of

Exeter. The first division, which can be extended to include the Isle of Man and Ireland, is often referred to as the *Highland* zone, since much of the area is of considerable elevation, often reaching a thousand feet and over. The south-eastern section, on the other hand, forms the *Lowland* zone since everywhere the relief is gentle; and although there are hills such as the chalk downs, they are generally smooth and low. This contrast is largely due to the nature of the rocks forming the two zones, as well as to the different processes they have undergone in the earth's history. In the north-west the underlying rocks are generally old and resistant, while in Lowland Britain they are newer and softer, being of Secondary or later ages. As a result, the soils of the Highland zone are often naturally thin and stony, demanding much toil to make them productive, whereas in the south-eastern division they are deeper and richer. There are, of course, significant exceptions to these general conditions; and in the Island may be picked out the areas surrounding Castletown as well as in the extreme north which are true lowlands with soils more fertile than those in other parts of Man.

The contrasts between the Highland and Lowland zones are also seen in the racial characteristics of the people, and in their ways of life and modes of thought. In the north-western area, which includes all of what is called 'Celtic' Britain, there has been a clinging to the earlier Celtic speech and the older culture; and even though the language has largely disappeared, there is nowadays a fresh interest in it, and in its associated stories and customs. The Lowland section, the stronghold of the English language and culture, has become the dominant area of Britain on account of its greater wealth and its closer connection with continental Europe, and English has spread northward and westward as Celtic receded. In this connection it is significant that the Island lies relatively close to south Lancashire which forms a north-westerly projection of the English Lowland, so that Man has been particularly open to influences from that direction.

The Celtic Fringe

Although in recent times the 'Celtic' area of Britain, which lies further away from the main streams of European life, has tended to become the more backward section economically, yet there have been periods when life was more vigorous there, and culture more advanced than in the south-eastern zone. Such a period, for example, was that known as the Megalithic phase, perhaps about 2,000 years or more before Christ (which will be discussed more fully in Chapter II), when trade was very active throughout the Irish Sea and along the western seaboard of Great Britain generally. Again, during the Early Christian period (from about 450 A.D. to 800 A.D.) it was the Celtic west, and particularly Ireland, that shone forth as the great centre of learning and of the arts. The Lowland zone during much of this time was being occupied by the Anglo-Saxons, who were still barbarians.

In the Highland zone, the old ideas and customs survived much longer; and foremost among them were the tribal customs which expressed the idea of kinship and clan. People thought not so much of a large community as of a fairly small one, a sort of big family with the chieftain as its father. The Isle of Man provides many examples of these ideas and customs, and much of its history will appear very puzzling unless this is remembered. As one illustration consider the use of white quartz stones which had some religious significance far back in pre-Christian times since they were used in the burial monuments of Megalithic peoples. They continued to be used after the introduction of Christianity, and they are found, for example, in the portion of the floor underneath the altar in one of the old ' keeills ' (or early chapels) in Maughold churchyard. Later on, white stones came to be associated with various superstitions and charms, and as such they continued to be used in recent times. They are, indeed, still used on graves, and as decorations on walls. Another example of a different kind is provided by the Tynwald ceremony which is held annually on July 5th. At one time it was believed that this ceremony was introduced solely by the Scandinavian conquerors of the Island; but although the actual name of Tynwald is Norwegian, and although many of the customs may owe their origin to the Norse, there can be no doubt whatever that the idea of an annual mid-summer assembly at St. John's goes back to a very early period in the history of the Island, and that this tradition has been kept up by Manx people right to the present day.

Another striking difference between the Highland and Lowland regions of Britain, which is very well illustrated in the Isle of Man, concerns the forms of settlement. In south-east England the typical unit tends to be the compact or nucleated agricultural village. One group of dwellings formed the nucleus, or core, from which people went day by day to work in the fields. But in the Highland zone, settlements are more dispersed or scattered, with single farmsteads surrounded by their fields forming the more characteristic units. The word 'Balla,' which is attached to so large a number of farms in the Isle of Man, often in conjunction with a personal name (e.g. Ballaclague, Ballamaddrell), indicates that the farm has been the home of a certain person and his family and dependents for many generations.

The General Physical Plan

The map of the Island's physical features shows that the central mass of the Island consists of a high plateau or moorland over 750 feet in height, (p.viii) above which rise a number of peaks most being over 1,500 feet. The most important line of such peaks extends from north-east to south-west, beginning in North Barrule, then through Snaefell, the highest of all (2,034 feet), on through Beinn y Phott, Garraghan, Colden and Greeba, whence the line is continued on the other side of the central valley between Peel and Douglas, in South Barrule and Cronk ny Irree Laa. This main axis is of great importance because it divides the Island into what were originally in many ways two distinct portions, the 'North' and the 'South,' whose significance will be discussed later. The actual boundary between these divisions can be traced by the main line of water-parting which is closely related to this belt of highlands although it does not usually follow the peaks themselves.

On the eastern and western sides of the central highlands the land usually takes the form of a lower plateau with an average height of about 400 feet. The best example is the belt running from Maughold, (Fig. 8), through Lonan and Onchan into Santan, although throughout this stretch the level is broken and glens are formed where the larger rivers cut across to the sea. On the western side of the Island a somewhat similar, if smaller, coastal plateau extends southwards from Kirk Michael.

Cutting right across the highland mass is the central valley between Douglas and Peel, which is followed by both a railway and a main road despite the narrowness in the middle, particularly near Greeba. Nowadays this valley is often regarded as the line separating ' North ' from ' South '; but in earlier days it was not so important partly on account of its narrow character, and partly because its floor was, and still is, swampy. Trackways from east to west formerly tended to keep to the higher ground outside the valley. On the other hand, at St. John's, where the valley is opening out towards Peel, is situated the most obvious meeting place in the whole Island, since routes from all directions—from the south via the Foxdale river, from the north via Glen Helen, as well as from east and west—converge at this point. From very early times, therefore, this has been the scene of a national assembly, and the spot has acquired a sanctity which has persisted right to the present day.

The Island contains two principal lowland areas:—(*a*) that extending north of a line between Ballaugh and Ramsey to the Point of Ayre, and (*b*) the smaller one surrounding Castletown in the south-east. The northern lowland is by no means uniform since it includes a low range of hills reaching over 300 feet, extending roughly east-west through Bride. The southern section of this lowland, where it borders on the main highland mass, forms the Curragh, (Fig. 5), and there were formerly a number of shallow meres extending from Ballaugh to Ramsey. These have now been largely drained, chiefly by means of the Sulby river, and the Killane and Lhen trenches, but they are still liable to flooding in the winter. Formerly, also, the Castletown lowland contained some stretches of water surrounding the Silverburn and in the Great Meadow, but these have also been drained.

The Chief Rock Formations

Three-fourths of the Island's area consists of hard slates and grits belonging to a very early period in the earth's history known as the Primary. These are the rocks that form not only the mountain mass but also the coastal plateaux, the only exceptions being the rather small but interesting areas made of igneous rocks, chiefly granite, including the Granite Mountain (near Foxdale) and also the quarries at the Dhoon and Oatland.

The grits and slates must have been originally horizontal, but owing to frequent earth movements since they were made, the beds have been twisted into various forms as may be seen in many quarries, and particularly around the headlands which provide such glorious coastal scenery.

In the Castletown lowland, on the contrary, the underlying rocks consist of beds of shale and limestone, which may be seen along the coast at Scarlet as well as in the Billown quarries. This rock has not only provided lime, so necessary for agricultural purposes, but it has proved a valuable building stone, as may be observed in so many of the houses as well as in the famous Castle Rushen. On the other side of the Island surrounding Peel, the local rock is a red sandstone which was also much used at one time for building houses and hedges, thus giving this district an appearance quite different from other parts.

The Glacial Period

It has been proved that rocks similar to the Castletown limestone and the Peel sandstone (which belong to roughly the same period in the earth's history) also exist far below the northern lowland; but they are covered by very thick deposits of what is called 'glacial drift,' consisting of soft clays, sands and gravels. These materials owe their origin to the great Glacial period which occurred only fairly recently in relation to the long history of the earth. Yet it ended about twenty thousand years ago, after having lasted for many thousands of years! During this Glacial epoch, it is believed that what is now the Irish Sea was filled with an ice-sheet which actually covered the whole of the Island, even over the top of Snaefell. This ice-sheet, which had come mainly from south-west Scotland and north-east Ireland, with some contribution from the Cumbrian region of England, carried with it rocks from all these lands as well as from the sea-floor. So when the ice covering the Island finally melted, it left behind a mixture of loose materials which can be seen in many parts lying on top of the rocks already existing there, while the whole of the present northern triangle of land was added as the result of such glacial action. During the later stages of the melting, great floods swept down from the highlands bringing much sand and gravel to the lower lands, such as may now be seen around St. John's and other places.

It can now be understood why, in many parts of the Island, pieces of rocks, actually called boulders, are found which, in a sense, do not belong to the Island but which have been brought during the Glacial period from Scotland, Ireland, or the Lake District. Perhaps the most striking examples are seen along the coast north of Michael, (Fig. 3), where many varieties of granite boulders occur, and where may also be found many pieces of flint from the chalk of northern Ireland, such as were used by early man to chip into arrowheads, knives, chisels and other objects. There are, of course, also many boulders from rocks within the Isle of Man itself which have been carried southwards by the ice; and the best examples of these are the masses of granite from the Foxdale Granite Mountain which can be traced right down to the Sound, and which have been used wherever available in buildings and hedges throughout the southern part of Man.

The Glacial period provided many of the soils on which agriculture depends both on the uplands and the lowlands. Above about 600 feet there is barely any soil cover; but below this, especially on the lower plateaux, there is usually a covering of glacial drift mainly derived from the local slates, and which, although stony, produces some fair crops. In the more fertile lowlands the deposits are generally deeper, and of a finer and more mixed nature. Of course conditions vary, especially in the northern lowland, where some of the sandy patches are too light and other clayey patches too heavy. An interesting feature of this lowland is the lack of suitable building stone from the solid rocks, so that much use has been made of glacial boulders for building houses and walls, such boulders often being obtained from the shore where they are very plentiful. Much of the stone in Bride Church consists of granite boulders originally carried by ice-action from southern Scotland. Bricks made from the local boulder clay are also more in evidence here than elsewhere on the Island.

Another interesting aspect of the glacial period is the appearance of the Irish elk or great deer (*Cervus giganteus*) whose remains have been discovered in various parts including St. John's, from which came the magnificent specimen with a spread of antlers extending to about nine feet, now exhibited in the Manx Museum. Most likely these animals first reached the Island across ice-fields when remnants of the great glacier still occupied the basin of the Irish Sea, and while the higher parts of the land were still emerging from the effects of the glaciation. They lingered on for some time before becoming extinct, but it is not quite certain whether they survived to the period which witnessed the growth of forests in the Island.

Finally, in the extreme north occurs a barren strip of shingle, known as the Ayre, having a width of about one and a half miles at its widest. This forms what is called a raised beach, now standing ten or twelve feet above the high water mark, while formerly it lay below it. It is important as indicating an uplift in the level of the land since the Glacial period. There are indications of a similar movement in the neighbouring regions of Scotland, Ireland and England, and the uplift seems to have occurred during the early history of man in the Island.

Chief Periods of Human History

There are two principal periods in the story of human development called the *prehistoric* and the *historic*, the difference between them being that in the case of the latter the evidence is based, for the most part, on written documents, whereas in the prehistoric period such written documents did not exist. Knowledge of that age is obtained from various relics left by man in the shape of domestic utensils (particularly pottery), ornaments, weapons, buildings and monuments of various kinds which are often associated with the burial of the dead. At the present day much valuable information concerning those far off days is being 'dug up' by very careful excavations, but it must be pointed out that this work is really only in its infancy and that there are still many gaps in our knowledge and many problems still waiting to be solved.

In Britain it is customary to regard the coming of the Romans in 55 B.C. as the dividing line between prehistoric and historic times, since it is with Caesar that there is a definite beginning of written accounts. But much of our knowledge even of the Roman period and also of the succeeding Anglo-Saxon period is obtained not from written documents but from the remains that have been dug up by archaeologists. As regards the Isle

Fig. 1.—Highland zone, with Snaefell slopes in background and deserted croft in foreground

Fig. 2—View from a point east of the Braaid showing the highland backbone from Greeba to Snaef

arraghan
Beinn
y
Phott
Snaefell
(in clouds)
Carn
Gerjoil

Fig. 3.—Glacial drift cliffs at Ballaugh and Jurby

Greeba
Mountain

of Man this date cannot be adopted since there is no evidence that the Romans settled in the Island, although they undoubtedly knew of its existence, referring to it under various names including Mona (Caesar, B.C. 54) Monapia (Pliny A.D. 23) and Mevania (Orosius, A.D. 416). The same is true of Ireland; and there the historic period may be said to begin about the middle of the fifth century A.D., or the period which marks the great extension of Christianity in that country as a result of the work of Saint Patrick. This same date may be adopted for the Isle of Man, since there is no doubt that it was deeply influenced by the same religious movement.

Thus the Island had a long prehistoric period beginning some thousands of years before Christ and extending up to about 450 A.D. From that date until about 800 A.D. there was what may be called the Early Christian period. Then followed the Scandinavian period when Man was conquered and colonised by the Vikings or Norsemen. This was a very important phase in the Island's history, despite the fact that it began with plundering and destruction and a partial return to paganism, since it brought a very virile people who proved to be good organisers and administrators. The Scandinavian period ended in 1266, three years after the defeat of the Norwegians by the Scots under King Alexander III. Then came a very confused and troublous time during which the Island was alternately under Scottish and English rule, until finally in 1405 it came into the hands of the Stanley family (later known as the Earls of Derby), who, with their connections the Dukes of Atholl, ruled it until the eighteenth century. Since 1765 the Island has had no independent ruler, but has come directly under the British Crown while still retaining its ancient constitution and the right to make its own laws.

Administrative Divisions (Fig. 4)

The Island is divided for the purpose of government into sheadings and parishes, there being six sheadings, all except one containing three parishes each. On the west, travelling from south to north, there are the sheadings of Glenfaba, containing the parishes of Kirk Patrick, Kirk German and Kirk Marown; Michael, with the parishes of Kirk Michael, Ballaugh and Jurby; and Ayre, with the parishes of Kirk Bride, Kirk

Andreas and Kirk Christ Lezayre. On the eastern side, passing from north to south, there are the sheadings of Garff, now containing only two parishes, Kirk Maughold and Kirk Lonan; Middle, with the parishes of Kirk Onchan, Kirk Braddan and Kirk Santan; and Rushen, with the parishes of Kirk Malew, Kirk Arbory and Kirk Christ Rushen*. Before 1796 the parish of Marown was included in the sheading of Middle, while Onchan was part of Garff. It is thus evident that the original boundary between the sheadings of the 'North'—Glenfaba, Michael and Ayre—and those of the 'South'—Garff, Middle and Rushen—was the line of water-parting following the main highland belt. This division existed not only on the map but in the minds of the people, and there were many points of difference between the 'Northside' and the 'Southside' dialects and customs. At present, with our quick and easy transport, it is difficult to realise how far it seemed from one side of the mountains to the other; but in early days the North and the South were like independent countries and they were occasionally in conflict as recorded, for example, in the year 1098. This feeling of separateness and remoteness is well expressed in one of T. E. Brown's verses in which he muses about *Braddan Vicarage*:—

I wonder if the hills are long and lonely
    That North from South divide;
I wonder if he thinks that it is only
    The hither slope where men abide,
Unto all mortal homes refused the other side.

Each region had its own capital, its own chief and various other officers connected with laws, defence and so forth. Where the original capitals were it is difficult to say—probably there have been various places—but in the end Castletown came to be the chief place in the South and Peel in the North; and when the Island was really united in one kingdom Castletown came to be the only capital until it was displaced by Douglas in 1869. One interesting survival of these two primary divisions is the fact that there are still two Deemsters,

*Here the full name of each of the ancient parishes is given, but elsewhere the prefix Kirk will be omitted. Onchan is used in preference to Conchan since the latter is tending to become archaic and is not, for example, used now in official notices. The name Arbory (after St. Cairbre) originally also had an initial C, but this has disappeared long ago.

or judges. Each division had its chief man of the law who has been known by different names at different periods. In pre-Norse times he was called the *Briw*, which was the name always used in Manx, but the Norse called him *Lagman* (or *Lawman*), and then the English introduced the term *Deemster*, the name which has continued until the present day. Until recently there was a Norther Deemster and a Southern Deemster, but since 1918 these officials have been known as the First Deemster and the Second Deemster.

The modifications in the administrative divisions introduced in 1796 had the effect of blurring the original significance of the terms North and South since it was decreed that, for legal purposes, the Northern district should include Michael, Ayre and Garff sheadings while the Southern district should include Glenfaba, Middle and Rushen sheadings. These divisions still hold good for the Common Law Courts, except that for some purposes Glenfaba is included within the Northern district. On the other hand, the Petty Sessions and the High Bailiff's districts are more modern and are based on the four towns and the parishes adjoining them. Hence with the borough of Douglas are included the parishes of Onchan, Braddan, Lonan and Marown. With the town of Ramsey are included the parishes of Maughold, Bride, Andreas, Jurby and Lezayre; while with Peel go the parishes of Patrick, German, Michael and Ballaugh. Lastly, with the town of Castletown go the parishes of Malew, Santan, Arbory and Rushen. These divisions also serve as districts for the Licensing Acts, and under the names of the Eastern, Northern, Western and Southern divisions they are often used at the present day for a variety of purposes. Individual Boards of Tynwald, e.g. the Highway and Transport Board, the Electricity and Water Boards, adopt other divisions which are more suited to their own particular needs.

Sheadings and Parishes

Nowadays the sheadings form electoral districts for the return of sixteen out of the twenty-four members of the House of Keys. There has been much dispute about the meaning of the name sheading, and the period when these divisions came into being. Some writers argue that the word means a 'sixth part,' and that it may be either Celtic or Norse. Others have

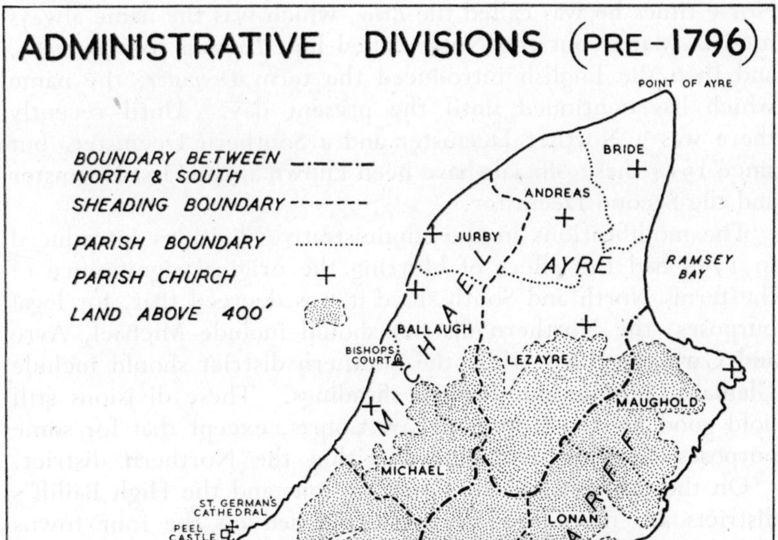

Fig. 4.—Administrative Divisions prior to 1796.

urged that it means a 'ship-division,' and that it was introduced by the Norse with the intention that each such district should provide a certain number of ships or war galleys (called *skeid* in Norwegian) for the service of the king. A more recent view is that the word sheading was derived from an old English word, *scheding,* meaning 'a division,' and that it was introduced by Sir John Stanley when he became King of Man in the early fifteenth century.

Whatever the precise origin of the word, there is reason to believe that the divisions which are now called sheadings originally corresponded with the chief tribal units of the Island. Each had its principal meeting-place something like a local Tynwald. During the Norse period these areas came to be better organised, and their boundaries more precisely defined, very much as they have persisted to modern times. It is quite likely, also, that the Norse introduced their custom of making each of the divisions provide one or more ships towards the defence of the Island. But the earlier functions of the sheading also continued, and these persisted for long after the Scandinavian period, since each had its own Sheading Court which settled questions concerning revenues and land tenures, while it also had power to deal with private disputes. Sheading Courts are no longer held, but all cases formerly dealt with in them are heard at sittings of the Courts of Common Law held regularly for the three Northside and the three Southside sheadings.

The divisions which are known as parishes were for long the basis of the military and civil organisation, as well as the religious life in the Island. Nowadays they are linked mainly with ecclesiastical and civil matters, but at first their function was probably more of a military character. Although precise proof is lacking, there is every likelihood that originally there were sixteen parishes—not seventeen as at present—each having a frontage on the seaboard. There is good evidence to prove that Santan and Marown were one. The centre of each parish was the church, and we find that almost every parish in the Island has the prefix Kirk, derived from the Norse word *Kirkja,* meaning church. When the parishes were created there were quite a number of *keeills* or chapels in each division, and the one that was selected to serve as the parish church was apparently that which occupied the most convenient site at the time, or for other reasons not so obvious such as some tradition of sanctity. This has sometimes meant that the parish church is now rather inconveniently situated for the parish as a whole, as in the cases of Maughold and Santan; but in other examples the church is placed more centrally, as in Rushen or Andreas.

Treens and Quarterlands

The divisions known as treens have given rise to a great deal of discussion, and all the problems connected with them have not yet been solved. The treens were fairly small units of land, usually varying in size from about 200 acres to 400 acres. In earlier days they formed quite important administrative divisions, especially for the fixing of land taxes, but nowadays these units hardly exist. It has been generally assumed that the word is of Celtic origin and that it has reference to the figure 'three.' But if it meant a third part of some bigger unit, nobody has ever discovered what the bigger unit was; while, on the other hand, the treen was not normally divided into thirds but into fourths, and in fact the name quarterland (or *kerroo* in Manx) is still used for these sub-divisions of the old treens. A more recent and very probable view is that it had a similar origin to the Celtic word *tirunga* ('ounceland'), used in the Hebrides for a land unit which the Norse in the Orkneys called *urisland*. Whatever the actual origin of the term, there is every likelihood that these units have had a very long history, and that they initially represented the areas of cultivated land which were occupied and developed for agricultural and pastoral purposes by individual families in very early days. Naturally the heads of such estates would be very influential men, and it is probable that they were the original freeholders who claimed the privilege of choosing the members of the House of Keys in olden times. Another interesting point relating to the former importance of the treen is that in the early days of Christianity in the Island (which will be discussed further in Chapter III), it appears to have been customary to build a small chapel (or *keeill*) on each of these units, which was maintained by the owner of the estate. Moreover, during Norse times, it is believed that each treen had the duty imposed upon it of supplying four fully equipped men, one from each of the quarterlands, to serve in the war-galleys.

Composition of the Population

It is obvious that the Manx population today is by no means uniform from the racial, that is to say the physical, point of view. Thus some people are very fair, while others are very dark, the latter being usually rather shorter in stature than the former. Certain districts tend to have rather more people of one type than of another, the northern parishes of Andreas, Bride and Jurby having a majority of fair-haired people, while Onchan, Braddan and Santan have a higher percentage of darker folk.

According to a survey made some years ago, the two most important race types found here are called the Mediterranean and the Nordic. People belonging to the first type have dark brown or black hair, brown eyes and a long narrow head, and are of medium stature. It is very probable that these first came to Britain before 2,000 B.C., during what is called the Neolithic period, from the western Mediterranean area via France; and although originally they were fairly widespread throughout the British Isles they are now chiefly found in the western fringes, including Ireland, Wales, Cornwall and the Isle of Man. Many, however, are also found in urban centres including London. In the Island itself these ' little dark people,' as they are often called, are found everywhere, but they are most numerous in Onchan, Braddan and Santan, while they occur as frequently as fair people in Rushen and Patrick. The Nordic type, which is distinguished by its fair hair, light eyes (usually blue), taller stature, long narrow head, long face and long narrow nose, came to the Island later, and its presence here is associated particularly with the Viking settlers. People of this type are now most frequent in the north, notably in Bride, Andreas and Jurby as well as in the southern parish of Malew. It is significant that these parishes contain the largest areas of fertile lowland, and it would appear that the Norwegians deliberately chose these richer districts for their own.

Naturally much intermixture has taken place in the course of time, and now many Manx people have blended characteristics, such as dark hair and light eyes, so that it is impossible to describe them as pure Nordics or pure Mediterraneans.

It is believed that the Island also contains some representatives of two other interesting types. One is distinguished by its tall stature, spare build, dark colouring, with a long and often very narrow head and face. It is sometimes referred to as the Plynlimmon type from the fact that it is usually found in the higher moorland areas of Wales and west Scotland; and the evidence seems to suggest that the type is very old, going back possibly to an early movement at the end of the Old Stone Age. The other type is broad-headed and dark, and strongly built. Men with these characteristics are found in certain coastal districts in Wales and along the western fringe of Britain generally. Some writers have suggested that these people came as traders or prospectors from the eastern Mediterranean to Britain, perhaps during the early Bronze Age.

There is one race type usually known as the Beaker, found fairly frequently in eastern Britain but apparently very rare in the Isle of Man. Beaker people are fair and tall but broad-headed, with strong brows and powerful faces; and, entering Britain from central Europe during the early Bronze Age, they brought with them the particular form of pottery known as beakers or drinking cups. Finds of these vessels in early burial mounds become less and less in going westwards from the eastern half of England and Scotland; and the fact that only one beaker has been found so far in the Isle of Man goes to prove that the Island was not affected very directly by either this culture or the distinctive physical type.

The Manx Language

The language which was formerly widespread in the Island but which decayed so rapidly during the past hundred years that it threatened to become extinct, is a branch of the Celtic group of languages, one of the oldest of the great Indo-European family. This also includes the Teutonic, Slavonic and Romance languages of Europe, as well as the languages of northern India.

Prior to the Anglo-Saxon invasions, Celtic in one form or another was the dominant language throughout the British Isles. Since then it has been pushed steadily westwards until now it persists only in western Scotland, Ireland, Wales and the Isle of Man. Within this Celtic area, moreover, there are two forms of the language distinguished as *q*-Celtic (or Goidelic) including Manx, old Irish and Scottish Gaelic, and *p*-Celtic (or Brythonic) including Welsh, the extinct Cornish, and Breton, the existing Celtic tongue of Brittany. According to some writers, *q*-Celtic is the older form which came from central Europe probably during the later Bronze Age, either across England and Wales or else directly from western France to Ireland. Then *p*-Celtic came as a later movement from continental Europe during the Iron Age, to be followed later on, as already seen, by English. Others think that the original form of Celtic to come to Britain was the '*p*' variety, while the '*q*' form only developed independently in Ireland a few centuries before Christ and then spread to the Isle of Man and western Scotland. The Manx form has been slightly influenced by Norse and later by English, which ultimately displaced it altogether as the common speech of the people.

REFERENCES:

FOX, CYRIL, *The Personality of Britain,* Cardiff, National Museum of Wales, 4th ed. 1943.

LAMPLUGH, G. W., *Geology of the Isle of Man,* London, 1903.

PYE, N., *Land Utilisation Survey Report on the Isle of Man,* London, 1940.

Manorial Roll of the Isle of Man, 1511-1515, translated by Rev. T. Talbot, Oxford Press, 1924. Amongst other things this valuable document illustrates the ancient divisions of the Island into North and South, and gives the names of sheadings with lists of treens, and names of property-holders in the early sixteenth century.

CUBBON, W., *The Treen Divisions of Man,* coloured plans based on the Manorial Roll, Douglas, 1937.

GILL, W. W., The Name 'Man' in Gaelic Literature, *Journal of the Manx Museum,* v. 1941; 'Eamhain' as a Name of the Isle of Man, *ibid,* v, 1942.

MARSTRANDER, C. J. S., *Treen and Keeill*, Oslo, 1937, also *Norse Conquest of the Isle of Man,* Oslo, 1932. Both books are in Norwegian but they contain summaries in English.

MARWICK, HUGH, Leidang in the West, *Proceedings of the Orkney Antiquarian Society,* xiii, 1934.

DAVIES, E., and FLEURE, H. J., Manx People and their Origins. *Journal of the Manx Museum*, iii, 1937. Also Report on an Anthropological Survey of the Isle of Man, *Journal of the Royal Anthropological Institute*, lxvi, 1936.

QUINE, J., *The Isle of Man*, Cambridge, 1911.

Chapter II.

PREHISTORIC TIMES

As already seen in the previous chapter, the stage of human existence called prehistoric is that which has left no ordinary written documents. Evidence of what happened in these days must therefore be gleaned from the actual remains of man himself and of his handiwork in the shape of weapons of stone, or metals, utensils (*e.g.* pottery), ornaments, and monuments of various kinds. Just how long this period lasted it is impossible to say, but it began at least five thousand years before Christ and ended, as far as this area is concerned, somewhere about the fifth century A.D. It should be stressed, nevertheless, that our knowledge of this period is, in many cases, still very slender, and it may quite well turn out that some suggestions which are put forward here will have to be given up or modified in the light of fresh facts that will be ' dug up ' in future years. All who are interested in these matters should watch keenly the results of excavations that are being made from time to time in the Island and elsewhere.

Divisions of the Prehistoric Period

The first division is that called the Palaeolithic, or Old Stone Age, when man was dependent on stones of various kinds (including flints) for making his weapons—fashioning them into various forms *e.g.* knives, chisels and scrapers, by patient and often very skilful chipping. People in that age had no knowledge of agriculture, but relied for their food on hunting and food collecting. So they could not make permanent settlements but were forced to lead some kind of nomadic or wandering life in search of food.

It used to be thought that the Old Stone Age was followed directly by the Neolithic, or New Stone Age, when man acquired a knowledge of agriculture and of the domestication of animals which ultimately enabled him not only to live a more settled or sedentary life, but in addition, to develop arts and crafts such as the making of pottery and weaving. It is now known that the Neolithic period was really separated from the Palaeolithic by what is called the Mesolithic, or Middle Stone Age, during which conditions of life did not show any marked advance on those of Palaeolithic times. It is also believed that this Mesolithic Age of north-western Europe was quite a long one extending perhaps from about 5,000 B.C. until, say, about 2,500 B.C. or even later. This would make the Neolithic Age only a relatively short one, since it is generally agreed that the next great division, called the Bronze Age, began in our area about 2,000 B.C. or some centuries later.

The Bronze Age receives its name from the fact that the metal called bronze, which is really an alloy of copper and tin, came into general use for the making of tools and weapons. But the use of stone axe-heads, flint knives and arrow-heads still persisted, especially in the poorer or more isolated districts. The Bronze Age saw further developments in agriculture and in pottery, while trade appears to have been quite active during much of this period, and such conditions led to the spread of ideas and to the development of culture.

The last big division of prehistory is called the Iron Age, and during it, bronze was gradually superseded by iron as the material for making weapons, although it remained in use for the making of ornaments. The use of iron spread into south-east Britain about 450 B.C., but probably some centuries passed before it had much influence on Man. Since Man had no definite Roman period, the prehistoric division of the Iron Age has to be carried on to at least about 450 A.D.

The Stone Ages—Old, Middle, and New

In the Palaeolithic Age climatic conditions must have been very severe, and for long periods the area was covered by vast glaciers and ice-fields which marked the stages of the great Ice Age. Although there is some evidence of early man in southern England at this period, it seems that he did not reach the Island. There is clear proof, on the other hand, that he arrived here during the next stage, that called the Middle or Mesolithic, which witnessed the spread of forests, first of pine and hazel, and later of oak with associated trees, over western Europe as a whole. It is probable that a wind-swept island like Man would be kept relatively free from forest, especially along its coastal margins, and it became much sought after by the fisher-hunting folk of those days. The first people of whom there is any definite knowledge were such primitive food collectors similar to those called Tardenoisians, living in England and other parts of western Europe at the same period. Most likely they reached the Island from north-west England nearly six thousand years ago. In Man, evidence of temporary settlements has been found in several coastal sites, such as Glen Wyllin and Cronk Urleigh in Kirk Michael, also on Peel Hill and the slopes near Ramsey; while in the south of the Island similar evidence has been found at Port St. Mary, Rhenwyllan, Poyllvaaish, Cass ny Hawin and Port Grenaugh. Probably a family, or a small group of families, settled for a season or so at each of these until they had exhausted the means of getting food. Finds have been made of quite small pieces of flint, called microliths, which have been deliberately chipped, and most likely they were fastened as barbs on wooden spears for use on hunting expeditions.

Later on in the Mesolithic period, or shortly after it, there is proof that another culture reached the Island. Flints of a different kind have been found on many of the sites used by the Tardenoisian folk, and also at places on the hills further inland, such as Kirkill, and on the slopes of Slieau Whallian. A very interesting feature about this culture is that it seems almost certainly to have come from northern Ireland, since the people chipped their flint implements in precisely the same way as folk living along the banks of the River Bann in Ulster. Since there cannot have been any land connection between these two areas at that time, it is evident that people must have been able to travel to and fro across this Channel in boats.

As time went on, more advanced ideas began to reach Man, including knowledge about the cultivation of the land so as to produce grain, and about the domestication of animals. Also the methods of making pottery and polished stone implements came to be acquired by the people, so that mankind passed gradually into that stage of development which is called Neolithic. How did these new ideas reach the Island? This is not yet known for certain; but it is known that the new knowledge developed first of all in the countries around the eastern Mediterranean and that it spread slowly to north-west Europe. It came partly overland across central Europe, and partly by sea through the Mediterranean, thence along the western seaboard of Europe via Iberia and France so as to reach Britain.

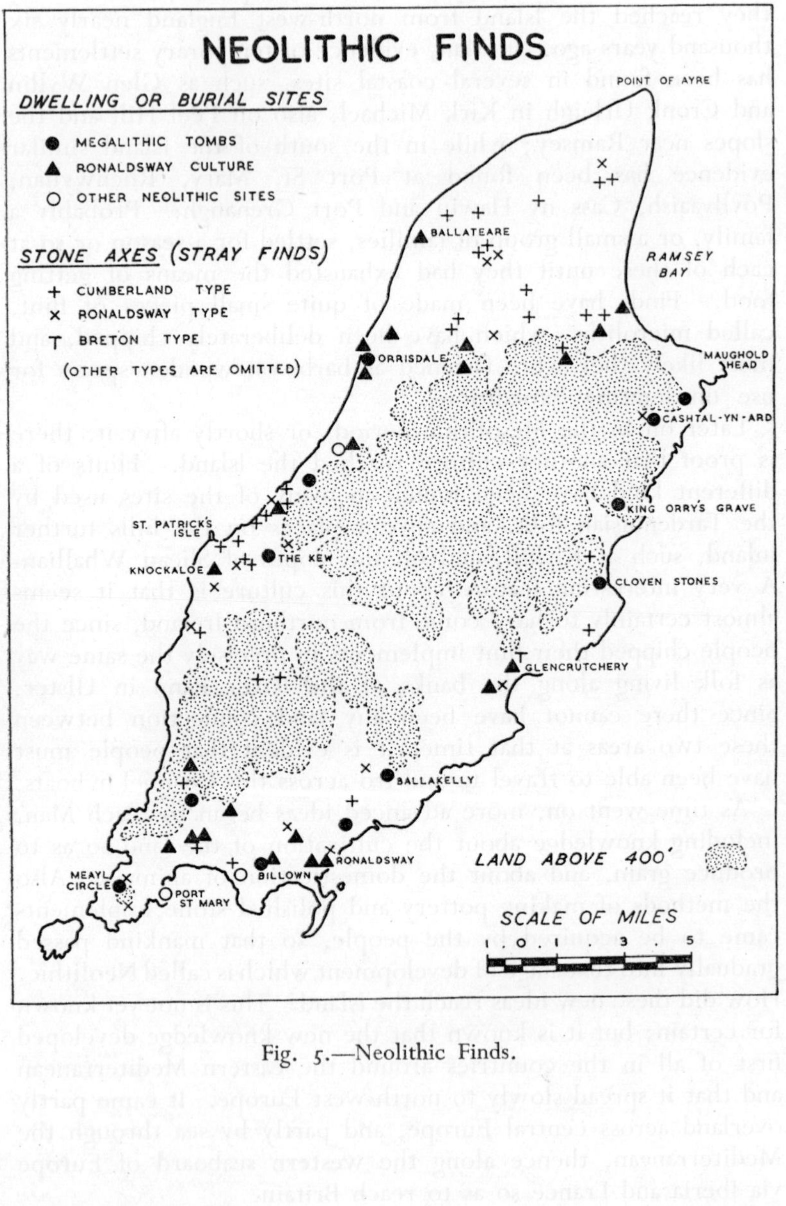

Fig. 5.—Neolithic Finds.

There are good reasons for thinking that it was by the latter route that the knowledge of agriculture and the pastoral life reached the Island. Firstly, it has already been seen in the previous chapter that most of the population at that period came from the western Mediterranean region. Moreover, there can be no doubt that sea-trade from the Mediterranean round the coasts of Spain, Portugal and France thence into the Irish Sea was going on during this Neolithic period, as it continued during much of the Bronze Age. Indeed, there is strong evidence that a trade-route which approached the Irish Sea in this way, continued on northwards by western and northern Scotland so as to reach Scandinavia and the Baltic.

It might be wondered why travellers from the western Mediterranean to the Baltic region did not prefer to go up the English Channel and via the Straits of Dover into the North Sea. There are various reasons for this, one being that the Straits of Dover may not have existed in their present form, probably being too narrow and dangerous. Moreover, south-eastern England, or the Lowland region of Britain as it has been called in Chapter I, was not quite as suitable for settlement then as it became later on, since much of the clayey land was covered with dense forest or was marshy.

On the other hand, the western part of Britain, including Man, offered certain advantages since many areas were not so heavily forested but were more open and so more attractive to early man. This Highland zone had further advantages which became more obvious in the Bronze Age, because it possessed greater supplies of copper and tin than the Lowland region, the former in Wales, western Scotland, and Ireland, and the latter in Cornwall. In addition, the fact that Ireland possessed supplies of gold, particularly in the Wicklow area, which human beings valued at quite an early stage, made that country a very great centre of attraction.

The Megalithic Culture

In the light of the conditions just sketched it is now possible to appreciate the significance of a highly important and interesting group of Manx monuments called *megalithic* because they are constructed of ' large stones.' Usually they are known by fanciful names such as the Druid's Circle, Cregneash, or

King Orry's Grave, near Laxey, or the Giant's Grave at Kew in Kirk German, and these names are apt to hide the true origin of the structures. Unfortunately many of these monuments have been so badly damaged, their stones having been removed to make hedges or houses, that it is now practically impossible to say what they were like originally. Happily, some have been better preserved and these are now being carefully guarded, while some have been excavated, such as the one known as Cashtal yn Ard, Maughold, so that we have a truer idea of their earliest form.

Most of these megaliths were certainly places for the burial of the dead, the remains being placed inside stone chambers (or cists). Sometimes only one or two such chambers survive, or there may be several of them arranged in some definite scheme as can be seen at Cashtal yn Ard, and the so-called Druid's Circle at Cregneash. There can be no doubt that the original idea of these collective tombs, and of the plans on which they were constructed, came from the Mediterranean, and that knowledge of them was brought along the western trade routes which existed during Neolithic and Bronze Age times. Thus, these monuments can be traced throughout the Highland zone of Britain where many of them belong to the later part of the Neolithic Age, others being constructed during the Bronze Age, while no doubt all of them continued to be used for some time after they were built.

In Man, these monuments are limited in general to areas between about 300 feet and 700 feet high (Fig. 5). They are almost entirely absent from the northern lowland, due possibly to the lack of suitable building stone there. On the eastern plateau running through Maughold and Lonan (Fig. 8) are three significant monuments having certain resemblances to one another, namely (1) Cashtal yn Ard, Ballachrink, Maughold, (2) King Orry's Grave, Gretch Veg, Lonan, and (3) the Cloven Stones, Garwick, Lonan. The first shows the essential features most clearly; and here, the burial chambers are arranged in the form of a long gallery, this gallery being approached from the western end through a crescentic forecourt, which is marked by a series of tall standing stones. (See Figs. 9, 10, 11). Originally, no doubt, the whole structure, apart from the forecourt, was covered by a bank of earth so that it would then

Fig. 6.—A landscape in the Curragh

Fig. 7.—Aerial view showing Snaefell and the Laxey River, also coastal plateau

Fig. 8.—Maughold Coastal Plateau (from Bulgham Bay)

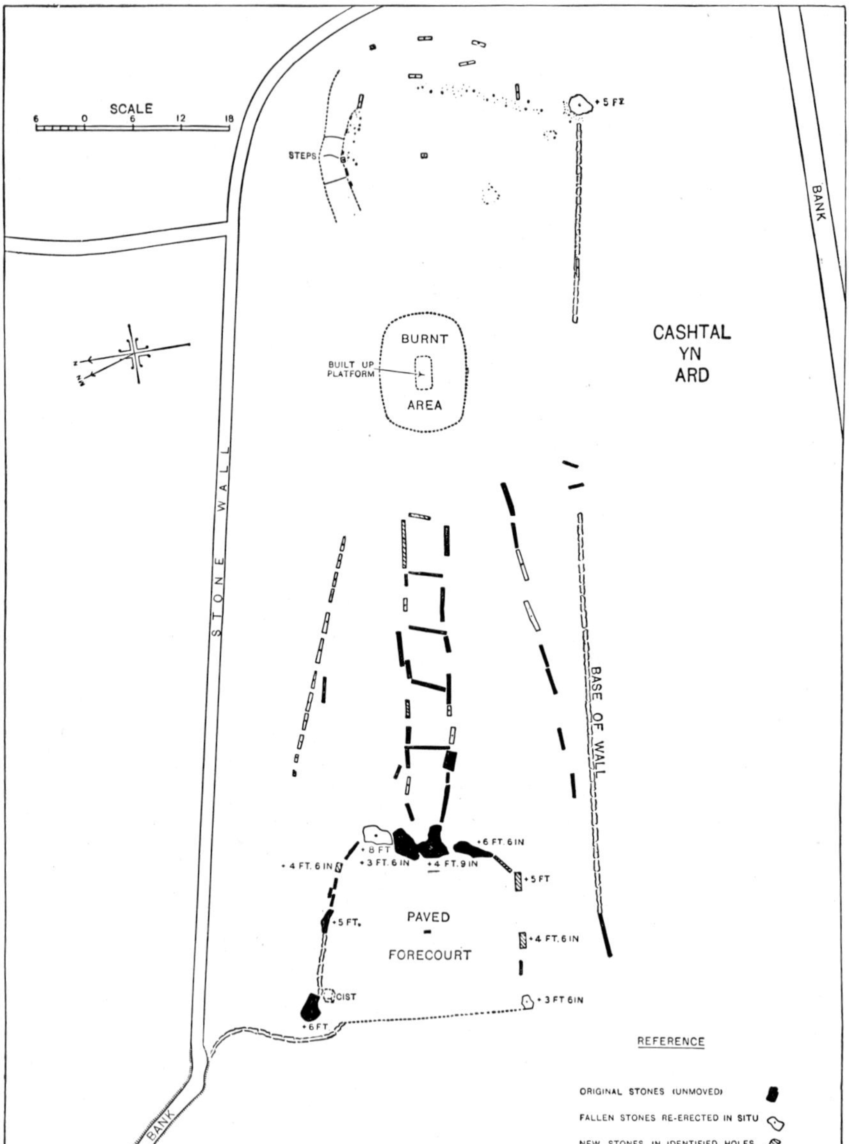

Fig. 9—Cashtal yn Ard, Maughold (Man)

Fig. 10.—Cashtal yn Ard, Maughold, (looking east) showing paved Forecourt and Porthole, beyond which is a Gallery of Cists

Fig. 11.—Cashtal yn Ard, Maughold, (looking west) showing Gallery of Cists

Fig. 12.—Beaker from Barroose, Lonan

Fig. 13.—Cronk Aust Food Vessel

have had the appearance of a long mound or horned cairn. Megalithic monuments of a very similar kind to these gallery graves are to be seen in adjoining countries, particularly in north-east Ireland and south-west Scotland, round the lower Clyde and in Galloway, thus indicating that these parts were inhabited by people of the same culture, and possibly ruled by members of the same tribe, or group of tribes.

In the extreme south near Cregneash is the Meayl Circle (or the so-called Druid's Circle), which is different in form from any other megaliths on the Island. It has six pairs of chambers arranged in a more or less circular form. Such a plan cannot be exactly matched elsewhere in Britain, so that the monument is very interesting as illustrating the development of a rather new type in Man, most probably at a late date in the megalithic period.

There are many other monuments consisting of just a single cist, such as the one near Tynwald Hill, about which little is known. Also, there are various circles of upright stones which do not seem to have any burial chambers associated with them. These stone circles are apparently limited to the British Isles and are not related to the Mediterranean area; but just what they represent and when they were built, are problems still to be solved.

Other Neolithic Finds

In addition to the megaliths which have just been discussed there are various indications of settlements of Neolithic age in many parts of the Island, both north and south, and occupying sites with a more distinctive lowland character. By far the most striking so far have been those revealed at Ronaldsway in the south-eastern lowland during the excavations in connection with the Airport in 1943. A unique feature here was the discovery of a primitive oblong dwelling house about 24 feet long by 12 to 14 feet broad with a hearth near the centre. The roof was no doubt held up by a series of wooden posts, the bases of fourteen such posts having been definitely traced. Within the house were considerable amounts of pottery, tools and bones; and the evidence seems to suggest that the site was occupied by a fairly large family group throughout a continuous period of time under what must have been relatively settled conditions. Stock-raising was apparently the chief occupation and the main source of food as indicated by the bones of cattle (including the Celtic shorthorn, *Bos longifrons*), sheep and pigs, especially the two first. Possibly the animals were kept at one end of the dwelling as in the characteristic ' long-house ' of many parts of western Britain in later days, while the human beings occupied the other end. Although there is no precise evidence of cereal cultivation at Ronaldsway, more definite indications of this have been found at Ballateare, Jurby, where a site dating to the same period of the Neolithic age has been discovered (Fig. 5).

Among the stone tools found in the Ronaldsway house were many polished axeheads up to 6 inches long, as well as smaller flint axes, adzes, saws and chisels, presumably used for tree-felling and carpentry. Other implements included stone hammers, flint scrapers and polished flint knives—used for dressing the hides and skins—as well as flint arrowheads. A fairly large amount of pottery was recovered, most of it very crudely made; and the more characteristic vessels appear to have been jars varying from 6 inches up to 16 inches across the mouth, with straight sides and round bases. Far from being ' cinerary urns ' as was formerly believed, these vessels are now thought to have been food storage jars kept inside the house for that purpose. Finally, possibly the most interesting finds at the site were five small oval-shaped slate plaques up to about three inches long and very thin, being only $\frac{1}{16}$ of an inch thick. Some of them show a lightly incised geometric ornamentation of chevrons and lozenges. So far nothing comparable to these decorated objects has been found in the British Isles, but the nearest parallels are the larger and more rectangular plaques of Portugal and Spain, while there are certain analogies, as far as the designs are concerned, with the Irish megalithic passage graves; and in both cases the links are with the Atlantic coastal routes whose significance has already been repeatedly stressed.

The Bronze Age

It has already been stated that this period began between 2,000 and 1,800 B.C. and that it lasted until a few centuries before Christ. The use of the metal was known in the eastern

Mediterranean much earlier, and it is quite probable that knowledge of it was brought along that same western sea-route by which had already come other new knowledge, such as the cultivation of grain. There was much activity in western Britain during the first part of the Bronze Age, particularly in Ireland, where there was a very extensive use of bronze. We have noticed Ireland's supplies of gold in the Wicklow area; while that country also had large supplies of copper, and was able to obtain tin easily from Cornwall.

Ireland attracted merchants from many countries and exported gold ornaments to France, Germany and Denmark as well as to England and Scotland. At least one piece of gold of Irish origin has been found in the Isle of Man, this being in the parish of Andreas. All of this activity must have affected the Island which stood as a convenient stepping-stone in the Irish Sea. The megaliths, which were described in the preceding paragraphs, must also have been in use during those times. Perhaps some were actually built then, and it is reasonable to suggest that they must have been used by groups of traders who were travelling about the Irish Sea a good deal at the time.

The Bronze Age may be subdivided into three periods, Early, Middle, and Late, during each of which it has been found that particular types of implements and also particular types of pottery were made. During the Early period, the typical bronze tools were flat axes of which at least half a dozen have been discovered in the Island, as at Surby in the south and at Andreas in the north.

As regards pottery, the most distinctive vessel belonging to this Early stage, at any rate in Lowland Britain, was the supposed drinking-cup called a beaker. This type was introduced into eastern England from central Europe by a broad-headed race very early in the Bronze Age; but so far only one beaker has been discovered in Man, at Barroose, Lonan (Fig. 12). On the other hand, at about the same period a type of pottery called the food-vessel—often very finely made and beautifully decorated—was being produced extensively in Ireland, and in other parts of the Highland zone of Britain. Three examples of these have been found in the Island, at Gretch-veg (Lonan), Bishopscourt (Ballaugh), and Cronk Aust (Lezayre), the last being a particularly fine specimen (Fig. 13).

During the Middle and Late Bronze periods, people made more elaborate kinds of bronze axes, called palstaves and socketed axes, which could be fastened more securely to their wooden handles, while bronze swords and spearheads also came into use. Examples of all have been found in various parts of the Island (Figs. 14 and 15). As far as pottery is concerned, the objects dating from these ages take the form of special types of burial urns in which the cremated remains of human beings were placed; and the Manx specimens that have so far been discovered have decorations very similar to those occurring in Ireland, thus indicating the persistence of influences from that country.

On the map on page 30, the sites of all the objects belonging to the Bronze Age which have so far been found in the Island have been marked, so that some idea is given of the areas in which there must have been fairly permanent settlements during the period. Clearly, the districts selected for such settlements were the fertile lowlands and the coastal plateaus within fairly easy access of the sea, and this is not surprising since here was to be found the land best suited to agricultural and pastoral development. The northern lowland had a relatively large number of settlements, in marked contrast to the period of megalithic culture when evidences of settlement are few.

Some of the higher lands were probably occupied temporarily during the summer season for grazing purposes as they were in later times, as well as for hunting; and it may be the case that the flint and stone tools which are found nowadays on the higher lands were used during the Bronze period for the latter purpose. No finds are shown in the central valley running between Peel and Douglas, and this might appear surprising in view of the existing importance of this route as the main link between east and west. But from what has been suggested in Chapter I, it is likely that physical conditions in this valley were not such as to attract settlements or routeways in earlier days. Thus the map serves to emphasise the extent to which the Island was separated by the mountain belt into two main divisions, the Northside and the Southside, which have been such an important feature in Manx life throughout much of its history.

For reasons which are not clearly understood, life seems to have deteriorated in the Isle of Man, and to some extent in Ireland and western Britain, towards the end of the Bronze Age, and for many centuries after. The climate seems to have become cold and wet during the eighth century B.C., and this may have diminished those trading movements which had kept up the current of ideas and had encouraged vigorous achievement. In this case it is easier to understand why there should have been a period of relative poverty in the Island. We must wait until further excavations have been made before we have any detailed knowledge of what conditions were really like during the period known as the Iron Age, and also during the first four hundred years of the Christian Era, when the Romans were occupying a good deal of Britain.

Early Manx Legends

There are a certain number of legends which seem to date from later prehistoric times and particularly from the Iron Age. These legends are essentially bound up with those of Ireland, chiefly northern Ireland, so that they indicate the continuance of that connection which has been shown to have been so strong during Bronze Age times. Moreover, these stories suggest trading and other links between Man and Ireland with the Western Isles of Scotland, thus pointing to a line of traffic which is known from other evidence to have been so important. The legends can be traced back to about the fifth century of the Christian Era, but they must previously have been handed down by word of mouth for many generations. It may, therefore, be suggested that they belong roughly to, say, the first century B.C. onwards, that is to the time when the knowledge and use of iron must have been slowly coming into the area.

The chief gods and heroes found in these myths are, of course, Manannan, as well as Conchobar, and Culainn. The first is often popularly supposed to have given his name to the Island, but it is much more probable that he obtained his own name from it; and perhaps it may be pointed out here that the actual name, which in Old Irish was written *Mana*, but which Caesar in B.C. 54 wrote as *Mona*, means ' mountainous ' or ' hilly land.' Manannan appears in the legends in so many different forms—as king, warrior, trader, navigator and

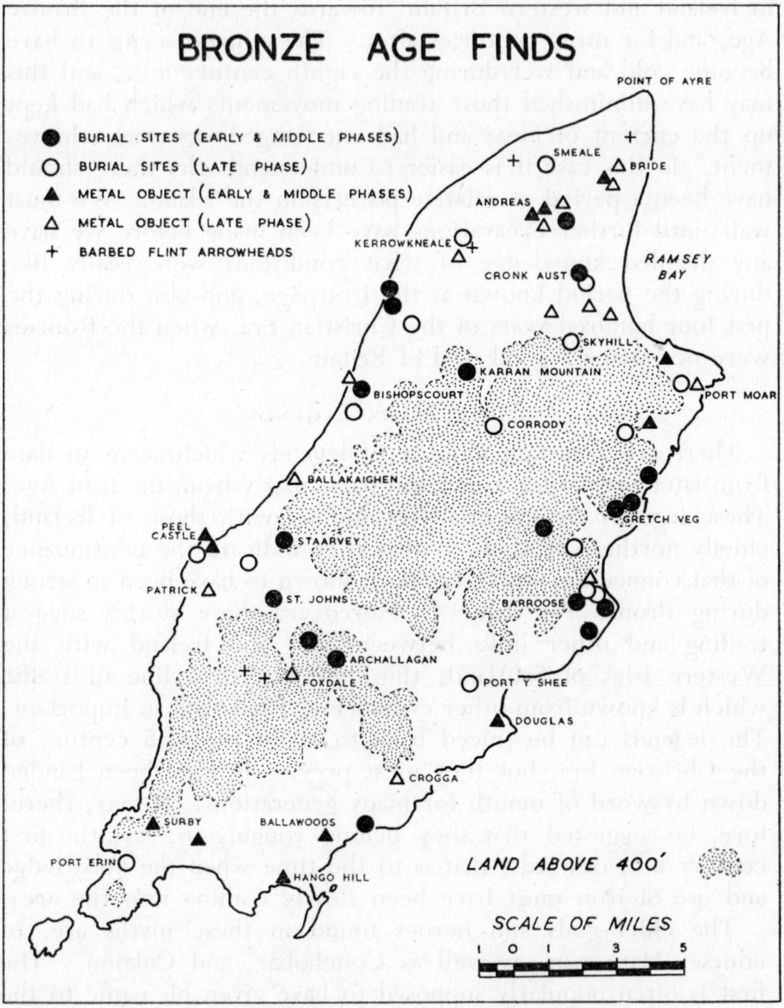

Fig. 14.—On this map the burial sites and metal objects found have been classified broadly according to age.

magician—that his original role can only be guessed at. He was, in any case, essentially bound up with the sea, whence he is often referred to as Manannan Mac Lir, that is, the ' son of the sea '; and probably the most interesting as well as the most likely explanation of his origin is that he reflected the vitally important part the Manx must have played in those early days as navigators and traders in the Irish Sea. Indeed, an Irish writer, Cormac, in the ninth century A.D., defines Mananann as ' a celebrated merchant who was in the Isle of Man (Manand). He was the best pilot that was in the west of Europe. He used to know, by studying the heavens, the periods which would be the fine weather and the bad weather, and when each of these two times would change.' This quaint explanation is probably as near as we are likely to get to the origin of the early Manx hero and god.

The exploits of Conchobar, a mythical king of Ulster, in his search for some wonderful weapons from Culainn, illustrate the link between northern Ireland and Man, but also serve to emphasise the importance of possessing good weapons of iron, such as were slowly coming into use in the area at that time. Culainn was, amongst other things, a famous smith and armourer, who is supposed to have lived for a time in Man, where he manufactured a sword, spear and shield of such amazing quality for Conchobar that the latter invited Culainn to go and live in Ulster. This great smith, according to the story, had some secret place of manufacture in Man, and he was persuaded to make the weapons for the ambitious young Conchobar through the intervention of a lovely young maiden whom the warrior found asleep on the shore when he arrived. Once in possession of the weapons, Conchobar was able to become king of Ulster while quite a young man. How far it is true that iron weapons of such quality were actually made in the Island must remain doubtful until other more definite evidence is forthcoming.

Other stories of later date have also been handed down concerning the exploits of a hero named Finn and his son Ossian. Finn is said to have been the chief of a band of soldiers, or robbers, called Fianns, who flourished in the second part of the third century A.D., and who had various adventures in northern Ireland, in Man, as well as in the Western Isles of Scotland. A Manx version of the story formed the subject of the oldest known composition in the Manx language; but unfortunately Finn appears to have become confused in this story with the much later Scandinavian hero, Orry or Gorry, who will be referred to in connection with the Norse period in Man.

Celtic Homesteads of Later Prehistoric Times

The Roman settlers in Britain knew that the Isle of Man existed, just as they knew of the existence of Ireland. A certain amount of trading, or perhaps of mere raiding, went on between Britain and Ireland in Roman times, because various Roman relics, including many coins, have been found in Ireland; and it is quite conceivable that traders with Roman Britain, or pirates who swooped down on the Romano-British coasts, made Man their centre. The only Roman finds so far seem, in any case, to be five coins, of which three were found in Castletown, one in the parish of Santan, and one in Onchan parish.

On the other hand, the progress of archaeological research since 1942 in the meadow land of the Dumb River at Ballakeigan, lying less than one mile north-west of Castletown, and at Ballanorris, Arbory, has revealed some very fascinating information regarding conditions on the Island during the first three centuries A.D. The site of the excavation at Ballakeigan consisted of two circular earthworks marked on the one-inch O.S. map as a 'Fort,' but, far from being anything in the nature of a fort, the structures that formerly stood there were two circular houses, each of which formed the dwelling place of a chieftain and his family, about, say, one thousand five hundred years ago. It cannot be said with certainty whether the two houses were occupied simultaneously, but they were very similar in plan, construction and purpose. The description which follows refers to the larger of the two sites (Figs. 17, 18).

This round, or 'Celtic,' type of house was quite large, having a diameter approaching ninety feet. The whole space was covered by a continuous and slightly domed roof made of sods. This roof is not likely to have been more than ten feet high at the centre, and it was supported by a series of massive oak posts which were arranged in five concentric rings. Remains of such posts show them to have been eight inches thick, and the trees from which they were made were, at that time, one hundred or even two hundred years old.

The outer wall of the house consisted of a continuous wall of posts of a similar size, hidden by a bank of earth heaped against it. Outside of this, about ten feet away, was a fence which prevented the animals from damaging the roof. A broad gap on the north-east opened on to a paved entrance-hall, and there was another smaller opening on the south.

In the centre of the house there was a large flat hearth, constructed of big slabs of Poyllvaaish limestone. Around the hearth were the living quarters, which were shut off from the rest of the house by a circular wattle screen supported by more slender posts of elm or pine. No doubt the remaining and much larger portions of the building were used for the stabling of animals in the winter, and for storage.

There is evidence that a certain amount of agriculture was carried on by the community occupying the house as some rotary granite querns have been discovered. Judging from the position of the settlement, however, it is quite likely that stock-raising was much more important as a means of livelihood. A large number of animal bones, including those of horses, cattle, pigs, sheep and goats, have been found here. Spinning and weaving were carried on, while crucibles containing glass have been found. Glass beads, blue, yellow and white, as well as bracelets, were worn as ornaments. A single amber bead was also found. Unfortunately, whatever iron implements were used have rusted away in the wet soil, but a few small ornamented bronze articles have survived.

From the evidence which has so far been gathered, this dwelling-house was in existence from about the third to the fifth century A.D., and it was certainly in continuous occupation by several generations of people of the same type. This long-continued use made renewals necessary from time to time, and there is evidence of three distinct changes of plan. The size of the house, the single hearth, and the character of the finds (despite their small number), all indicate occupation by a family of social standing comparable to that held in England, in later years, by the squire in his manor-house. Since there appear to be a number of such sites in the Island, the existence of numerous local chieftains seems to have been a feature of the insular social organisation in this phase of Celtic times.

The house was quite unfortified, and this is a very interesting point, since it indicates that a prosperous family was able to live in peace without special protection, despite the fact that they were so close to the sea and a landing place. Houses of essentially the same plan no doubt existed also on the higher lands where supplies of stone were more plentiful. In these cases the outer bank of earth would be faced with stones, and circles of such stones would then form the last visible remains of what were originally earth-roofed houses. Thus, there is every likelihood that the stone circle at the Braaid, which has hitherto been regarded as a megalithic monument, really represents the site of a Celtic round house similar to, but smaller than, that at Ballakeigan. Excavations of a mound known as 'The Round Table,' near Ballanorris, Arbory, show that yet another type of earthwork, resembling the remains of a medieval motte, has proved to be a round house of sixty feet diameter of the same type and age. It thus appears that these Celtic round houses were rather common in the Island.

Finally, it should be noted that similar monuments occur in Ireland, where they are usually referred to as 'raths.' In Scotland, too, the small 'duns' are very similar, and it would seem that in other parts of western Britain, including Wales, social conditions prevailed closely comparable to those in Man. It is of no special importance that many such constructions occupy sites possessing natural defensive advantages. It may be concluded from the knowledge gained by the excavations, that the period in question, which marks the close of prehistoric times in Man, was one of internal quiet and peaceful development, and that the Island was not then menaced by raiders from other lands immediately adjoining the Irish Sea.

A result of general interest arising from these excavations is that we now know what the houses of the knights and 'kings' of the later Celtic times were like. It is such round houses as these that we must probably picture to ourselves as the dwellings of the heroes of the Golden Age of Arthurian romance. The impermanence of their wooden construction has afforded only a glimpse of their lay-out, but the very character and complexity of that lay-out give grounds for the belief that they were at least equally elaborate in their fittings and ornamentation.

REFERENCES

NOTE.—For actual specimens of flint implements, food-vessels, bronze weapons, etc., reference should be made to the Manx Museum.

CLARK, GRAHAME, Prehistory of the Isle of Man, *Journal of the Manx Museum,* III, 1936; also *Proceedings of the Prehistoric Society*, I, 1935.

KERMODE, P. M. C., The Ancient Monuments of the Isle of Man, *Archaeologia Cambrensis,* lxxxiv, 1929.

KERMODE, P. M. C., *List of Manx Antiquities,* Douglas, 1930.

MEGAW, B. R. S., Manx Megaliths and their Ancestry, *Proc. I.M. Nat. Hist. and Antiq. Soc. (new series)*, IV, 1937.

FLEURE, H. J., and NEELY, G. J. H., Cashtal yn Ard, *Antiquaries Journal,* xvi, 1936.

KERMODE, P. M. C., and HERDMAN, W. A., *Manx Antiquities,* Liverpool, 1914.

CHILDE, V. GORDON, *Prehistoric Communities of the British Isles,* London, 1940.

NEELY, G. J. H., Excavations at Ronaldsway, *Antiquaries Journal*, xx, 1940.

MOORE, A. W., *Folklore of the Isle of Man*, Douglas, 1891.

FLEURE, H. J., and DUNLOP, M., Glendarragh Circle, The Braaid, *Antiquaries Journal,* xxii, 1942.

BERSU, GERHARD., Celtic Homesteads in the Isle of Man, *Journal of the Manx Museum,* V, 1945-6.

Chapter III.

THE EARLY CHRISTIAN PERIOD

(450-800 A.D.)

The period between the fourth and ninth centuries was of great importance to western, or Celtic, Britain since it was then that Christianity first took root and flourished. As in the case of earlier cultures the religion seems to have penetrated via the Irish Sea, touching on all its fringing lands; and from this area of Highland Britain missionaries were in time sent eastwards to continental Europe. On the other hand the Lowland zone, during the earlier part of this period, was thrown into confusion following the withdrawal of the Romans and the invasion of the Anglo-Saxons; and ultimately Christianity was introduced afresh into south-eastern England by the famous mission of St. Augustine in 597 A.D.

As far as Man is concerned, there is a tantalising lack of direct information relating to this fascinating age, although much more is known concerning Ireland. If any records existed in Man they have disappeared, perhaps being destroyed by the Norsemen who destroyed so many books in Ireland too. We are, therefore, forced to rely on other sources of information, such as the remains of ancient chapels or keeills, with their dedications, and the cross-slabs, while we cannot neglect the various legends that have been handed down from ancient times.

Ogham Stones

Before dealing with the actual beginnings of Christianity in Man due attention must be given to those memorials called Oghams, which were at one time thought to be Christian tomb-stones, but are now considered to have been originally pagan, although in some cases they may have been used by Christians after the addition of the symbol of the cross.

In the Ogham script each letter is formed by a certain number of strokes cut on the stone, and it is known that such a method of writing was developed in southern Ireland, probably during the fifth century A.D. (Certain letters of the Ogham alphabet

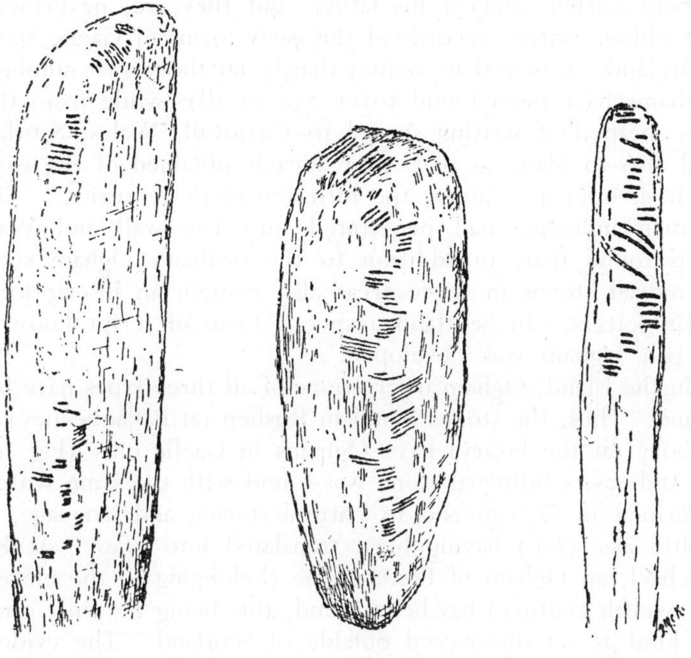

1. 2. 3.

Fig. 15.—Ogham Inscribed Stones. Nos. 1 and 2 from Ballaqueeney, Rushen, No. 3 from the Friary, Arbory.

Translations:—

1. (The stone) of Dovaidu, son of the Druid
2. (The stone) of Bivaidu, son of the clan of Conavali (i.e. Connell).
3. (The stone) of Cunamaglus, son of . . .

Note.—Another stone was found at the Friary bearing the name *Magleog*, which is the same as the modern Clague.

are depicted on the third line of characters shown on Fig. 28). There is much reason for believing that this script was originally invented as a system of secret signs, made with the fingers and used by the druids, or high priests of the old pagan religion, to enable them to converse with one another in a manner which was unintelligible to the ordinary people. The inscriptions on such stones usually give nothing more than the name of the person buried, and of his father, but they are, nevertheless, the oldest written records of the early forms of Gaelic spoken in Ireland. It is in that country that by far the largest number of Oghams have been found (over 250 in all), while from there this method of writing spread to Cornwall, Wales, Scotland, and also to Man, so that some idea is obtained of the extent of Irish influence during the fifth and sixth centuries.* Since Roman influence had penetrated into Cornwall and Wales, it is found that, in addition to the ordinary Ogham script, memorial stones in those areas also contain an inscription in Latin letters. In Scotland a special form of script known as Pictish Ogham was developed.

In the Island, Ogham inscriptions of all three types have been found. Thus, the stones found in Rushen (at Ballaqueeney) and Arbory (at the Friary) have Oghams in Gaelic only (Fig. 15). In Andreas, a bilingual stone was found with the same wording inscribed in Ogham and in Latin lettering and language, the Celtic *mac* (son) having been translated into *filius*. At Kirk Michael, an Ogham of Pictish type (belonging to the eleventh or twelfth century) has been found, this being the only one of its kind as yet discovered outside of Scotland. The evidence suggests, therefore, that there was a fair amount of movement of peoples and ideas across the Irish Sea during the fifth and succeeding centuries. Such intercourse must account to a considerable extent for the spread of Christianity throughout Celtic lands during this early period, and it seems evident that Man formed a natural cultural focus in the Irish basin from north, south, east and west when the sea routes were dominant.

Early Christianity in Britain

There is definite proof that Christianity existed in Britain in the fourth century, that is, during the Roman occupation of south Britain. The new religion seems to have influenced particularly the western parts of Britain, including Cornwall and Wales, and also south-western Scotland where St. Ninian, who died about the year 432, built a famous church at Whithorn on Wigtown Bay, towards the end of the fourth century. Parts of Ireland were also affected by these early movements since it

*For map showing distribution of Oghams, see, Fox, *Personality of Britain*, p. 43.

is certain that there were some Christians in that country before St. Patrick went there.

The Great Celtic Saints: St. Patrick and St. Columba

Although everyone associates St. Patrick with Ireland, he was really not an Irishman by birth, since he was born in the Roman province of Britain about the year 389. He was educated as a Christian by his father, who was a local Roman official. When only sixteen years old Patrick was carried off to Ireland by a band of raiders. After being in captivity there for six years he escaped in a boat trading from the coast of Ireland, and was carried to western France, or Gaul as it was then called. Here he came into contact with educated Christians, and after some years he returned to his home. But his experience in Ireland filled him with a strong desire to go as a missionary to help the Christians already there, and to extend the new religion, especially in the north where the druids had great power. About the year 432 therefore, he set off to Ireland as a bishop; and between that date and his death in 461 he accomplished his great work of spreading the faith and organising the Christian Church in the land to which he had first gone as a slave.

Schools were established in Ireland and learning was encouraged, so that many scholars were trained, several of whom went forth as missionaries to carry their faith and their learning to other lands surrounding the Irish Sea. The best known was St. Columba who was born in Donegal in 521. He had great influence not only on account of his piety and ability, but also because he was related to the royal family of Ulster and to the ruler of that part of western Scotland then known as Dalriada, but now called Argyll. Columba undertook the task of converting the Picts of highland Scotland, and for this purpose he established, in 563, the famous monastery on the island of Iona off the west coast of Mull (see map, Fig. 24). This hallowed spot, 'by the salt main on which the sea-gulls cry', became the great centre from which Columba and his disciples made many journeys, not only to the far north of Scotland but also to the Anglian kingdom of Northumbria and to Man, so that by the time of the Saint's death in 597 Christianity had spread far and wide throughout western and northern Britain.

Celtic Christianity in Man

It is quite obvious that the Island was deeply influenced by all these missionary movements, although there is no precise record that any of the three famous saints visited Man, nor is it known just when Christianity was introduced here.

St. Ninian's church at Whithorn is very close to the Island, and his name survives in the name of St. Trinian's (a corruption of Ninian), which is given to an old church in Marown where the Priory of Whithorn for long held lands.

St. Patrick's name is widely honoured, being used for two parish churches (Kirk Patrick itself, and Kirk Patrick of Jurby) and also seven keeills, apart from various sacred wells; while it is associated with the two upright stone pillars bearing early Christian crosses, known as St. Patrick's Chair, in the parish of Marown. There are various legends that the Saint actually visited the Island, but definite proof of this is lacking.

Many Manx churches and keeills are named after other Celtic saints who are supposed to have lived in Ireland during St. Patrick's time, or not long after. They include Machud (who gave his name to Maughold), Lonan, and Bridget, 'the holy head of Ireland's nuns,' who gave her name to the parish of Kirk Bride as well as to several keeills. Other parishes whose names are derived from Irish saints are Arbory (from St. Cairbre), Santan (from St. Sanctan), Braddan (from a saint whose name is spelt in various ways including Brendan and Braddan), Onchan or Conchan (from St. Conchenn), and German (from a saint of the same name). Lastly, the parish church of Arbory is also dedicated to St. Columba; and *Laa Columbkilley*, or St. Columba's Day, is still held as a fair day in the parish, having been revived in modern times. A keeill in Kirk Andreas is also dedicated to St. Columba. One of Columba's disciples was known as Molua or Moluoc, and it is to him that the parish of Malew is dedicated; while Marown is dedicated to Ronan, who was later than Columba but belonged to the Columban church.

The Keeills

Possibly the very earliest churches in Man were built of sods, or of wattle and mud, and there is now no trace of them.

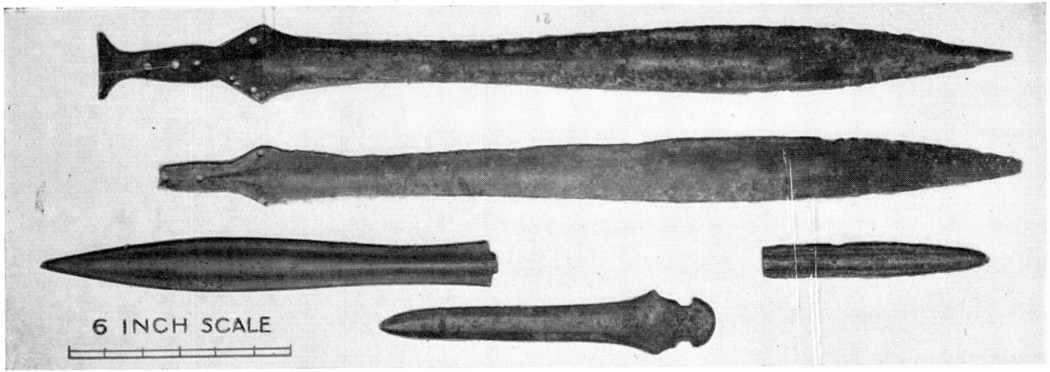

Fig. 16.—Bronze Swords in the Manx Museum

The uppermost Leaf-shaped Sword came from Berrag, Jurby; the one below from Crogga, Santan; both about 1,000 B.C. The Leaf-shaped Blade came from Foxdale; the broken Blade from Peel Castle; and the lowermost Dirk came from the site of the old Post-office, Athol Street, Douglas.

Fig. 17.—Celtic Round House—Section

Fig. 18.—Reconstruction of the Celtic Round House recently excavated at Ballakeigan

Fig. 19.—Irish Oratory

Fig. 20.—Ruins of Sulbrick Keeill, Santan, after excavation

Graves have been found together with crosses which scholars ascribe to the fifth century, and it is probable that they mark the sites of buildings which have disappeared. Later on stone buildings were erected, the stones at first being held together with earth. Afterwards clay was used as a cement, and finally lime or shell-mortar. The foundations of many of these structures still remain, now being carefully preserved by the Manx Museum Trustees. They date from the seventh to the fourteenth centuries. They were simple structures and usually quite small, the keeill at Lag ny Keeilley on the seaward slope of Cronk ny Irree Laa being, for example, only 13 feet long and 8 feet 6 inches wide (Figs. 19 and 20). The simple rectangular plan, with no apse or rounded end, and with no clear division between the nave and the chancel, became a kind of ' Manx style ' in church-building, and may still be seen in many of the existing parish churches.

The earliest keeills, being so small, could not have been intended for congregational worship but rather as places in which the first Christian missionaries could offer up their simple service of prayer and praise. Preaching would have been conducted out of doors, and so too would baptism, for a holy well, or *chibbyr*, is usually found near these old chapels. Many of the keeills that have been examined are known to have been built on sites that had been sacred for a long time previously, thus illustrating that respect for tradition which was noted earlier on (page 3) as a marked characteristic of the Celtic area of Britain.

So far some 200 keeill-sites have been discovered in Man, all districts being represented except the higher mountain lands and the marshes. As previously stated there appears to have been one on every treen, and a very recent survey shows that about 174 of such treen-chapels are known to have existed. Most probably the Celtic missionaries had a small church set up on each family estate, or treen, to counteract the influence of ancestor-worship which had previously existed. Also the people gradually gave up worshipping the various pagan gods such as Lugh, the great sun god, Ler, the god of the vast ocean, and Manannan, the god of wind and storm and mist, who had formed the chief dieties of the Celtic world.

The Arts during the Early Christian Period

Accompanying the great religious movements there were vitally important developments in learning, as well as in the arts and crafts. In Ireland the period from about 650 to 800 A.D. is spoken of as the Golden Age. Beautiful things were created in architecture, metal work, the illumination or adornment of the pages of sacred books, and in sculpture. Man contains no examples of the first three of these arts, possibly because of its smallness and relative poverty in natural resources. In sculpture, on the other hand, notable progress took place, and a fine collection of inscribed and decorated monuments has been the result. Copies of these monuments, in plaster-casts or in drawings, form one of the most valued departments of the Manx

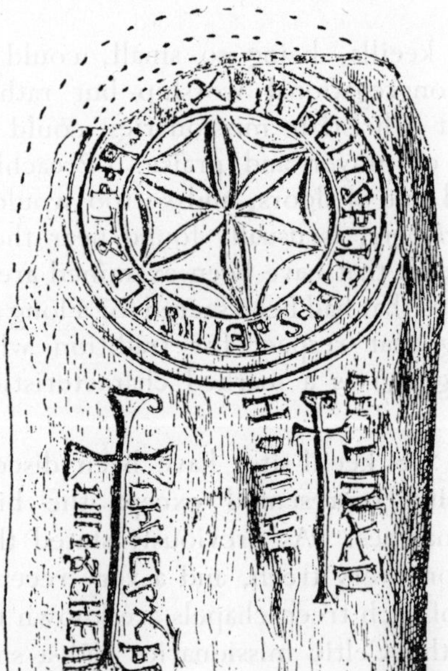

Fig. 21.—An early Cross from Maughold

Museum. As will be seen later, this form of art was continued and improved upon during the Scandinavian period, so that the Island is very fortunate in posesssing a wonderfully rich series of stone crosses. The task of collecting, interpreting, and arranging this famous collection was accomplished by the late Mr. P. M. C. Kermode, who described the stones in his great work entitled *Manx Crosses*.

Earliest Manx Crosses

As already seen, the first inscribed stones in the Island are pagan, and are marked merely with Ogham characters belonging to the fifth and sixth or succeeding centuries. As Christianity made its influence felt, slabs of stone were engraved with simple representations of the cross and set up as memorials to the dead. The earliest of these date to the fifth or sixth centuries, and some twenty examples of this age have been found in different parts, four being from the ancient burial ground surrounding the keeill at Lag ny Keeilley. Improved workmanship is evident in a specimen probably dating from the early eighth century, and found at Maughold, that famous old centre whose sanctity extends from megalithic times to the present day. This stone contains a circle enclosing an hexagonal design, while inside the circle is a Latin inscription which is very difficult to interpret. It was formerly thought to refer to a certain ' Itspli ' as ' Bishop of God in the Isle(s),' but this can hardly be accurate since there was no diocese of the Isles before the twelfth century. The more modern view is that it commemorates someone named ' Irneit ' (or Irneitus), a ' Bishop from Iona,' although no bishop of that name appears to be otherwise recorded. Below the circle are two smaller Christian crosses of a very rare and early type, with the inscription reading:—' In the name of Christ a figure of the Cross of Christ.' An interesting feature here is that while the monogram is in Latin some Greek letters are used, including the H in place of the Latin N, showing that Greek letters were familiar to the carvers of these monuments. (Fig. 21).

One of the earliest examples of the type known as the Celtic cross, with a circle surrounding the form of the cross, is a stone from Ballavarkish, in Bride, which dates to the seventh century. Many stones of this type were produced, some with wonderful designs and workmanship. A cross dating to the later eighth century, and depicting the Crucifixion, has been found on the Calf of Man (Fig. 22). The workmanship on this is considered to be finer and more delicate than that on any other known stone of the same period. Several Manx crosses of this age have designs and lettering which may have been influenced by similar ones from Northern England, indicating that there were some connections between Man and the Anglian kingdom of Northumbria.

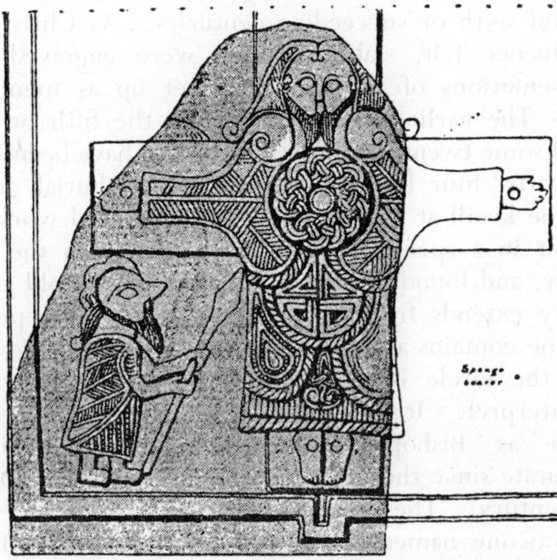

Fig. 22.—The Calf of Man Crucifix

Summary

Although there exist no ordinary historical records of the period between 450 and 800, no lists of spectacular events, and no names of great men, it must not be supposed that the land lay in darkness. On the contrary, trade and cultural relations were maintained with Ireland, Scotland, northern England and Wales. Christianity spread over the whole Island, and the foundations were laid of that art which produced the exquisite Manx crosses.

REFERENCES

MACALISTER, R. A. S., *Archaeology of Ireland*, London, 1928.

KERMODE, P. M. C., *Manx Crosses,* London, 1907.

BURY, J. B., *Life of St. Patrick*, London, 1905.

PORTER, A. K., *The Crosses and Culture of Ireland,* New Haven, 1931.

ADAMNAN, *The Life of St. Columba,* Dublin, 1857.

SIMPSON, W. DOUGLAS, *The Celtic Church in Scotland,* Aberdeen University Studies, Aberdeen, 1935.

O'KELLEHER, A., and SCHOEPPERLE, G., *Life of Columcille,* Chicago, 1918.

KNEEN, J. J., *Place Names of the Isle of Man* (6 vols.), Manx Society, Douglas, 1925 to 1929.

MARSTRANDER, C. J. S., *Treen and Keeill,* Oslo, 1937; also see article in *Journal of Manx Museum,* iv, 1938, (including map of the Keeills).

BOWEN, E. G., Early Christianity in the British Isles, *Geography*, xviii, 1932; also, The Travels of the Celtic Saints, *Antiquity*, xviii, 1944; also, Settlements of the Celtic Saints in South Wales, *Antiquity*, xix, 1945.

The Manx Archaeological Survey, Douglas, five reports from 1909 to 1918, giving full details regarding the excavation of the Keeills.

CHAPTER IV.

THE SCANDINAVIAN PERIOD
(800-1266)

THE KINGS OF MAN AND THE ISLES

THE COMING OF THE NORSEMEN

TOWARDS the end of the eighth century the era of quiet prosperity which has been described in the previous chapter was shattered by the coming of the Norsemen from Scandinavia. Those great sea-warriors were also called Vikings, the usual derivation of the name being from the numerous creeks and bays along the Scandinavian coast known as fiords or *viks*. A more modern theory favoured by some scholars is that the term really has reference to the fact that these people were absent from home for long periods on raiding or other expeditions.* At first they were known as peaceful fishermen and traders. Then, encouraged by the unsettled conditions prevailing in their own country and in other countries of Europe at the time, they became pirates, harrying the coasts of Britain and western Europe, even penetrating the Mediterranean to Italy and Sicily. In eastern Europe they followed the great rivers into the heart of Russia and ultimately reached the city of Constantinople.

The Scandinavians included three groups of peoples, Norwegians, Swedes and Danes, but only the Norwegians (or Norse) and the Danes came to Britain in large numbers, since the Swedes were mainly interested in eastern Europe. As to the area of the Irish Sea with which we are particularly concerned, it may be stated that the people who came were almost wholly from Norway, particularly the south-western districts of that country. The Danes made settlements on the eastern side of England, and some went round the south and so got into the Irish Sea that way, but since only a few groups did this they can be disregarded.

VIKING SHIPS AND WARRIORS

The arts of ship-building and seamanship were more advanced in Scandinavia than in other parts of Europe at the time, so

*From Scandinavian word *vikja* meaning, 'not to follow the straight line,' 'to make a digression.' I am indebted to Prof. J. Bronsted, of Copenhagen, for this derivation.

that its peoples were able to accomplish the long journeys for which they were very famous, not only to Britain, but also to far-off Iceland and Greenland, and even to America itself. Much is known of their ships not merely from old Norse stories, or *sagas* as they are called, but also from the remains of actual ships. It was a common custom for a chief to be buried in his ship, the whole 'grave' being covered with a mound or *how*; and several such vessels have been discovered, two of the most famous being those of Gokstad and Oseberg on Oslo Fjord. An accurate model of the former can be seen in the Manx Museum, and an illustration is given in Fig. 23.

Fig. 23.—Model of Viking Ship from Gokstad, Norway

The ships were shallow, narrow in the beam, and pointed at both ends, and thus were very suitable for handling in creeks and bays, while they could easily be run up on the beaches. Each ship had but one large and heavy square sail, and when a naval battle was in progress it depended for its movement on the rowers. The number of the latter varied with the size of the vessel, but on the average each ship had ten rowers on either side. Since these ships would often have to be rowed both day and night against a contrary wind many more men would be needed, while others would be required to fight. Thus, for a vessel of twenty oars something like sixty men would be necessary. The Gokstad ship was an oak vessel with seats for sixteen pairs of rowers, and was 78 feet long and 16 feet broad amidships. Vessels carrying up to sixty pairs of rowers also existed.

As is known from various representations (as for example, the Bayeux Tapestry), the decorated shields of the warriors hung outside along the bulwarks, and the vessel was steered by an oar on the right, or starboard side. The bow and stern rose high, and the bow looked grim, being carved as a serpent's or dragon's head.

The warriors were well armed. For defence they had a helmet, mail-shirt of iron rings, leather or thick wool clothing, as well as a light round shield with an iron boss in the centre. For offensive purposes they used a sword, spear or battle-axe.

These Norsemen were strong and fearless on both sea and land. The thrill of battle gave them immense joy, and they believed that open plundering was honourable, although to steal secretly was shameful. Such were the men who controlled Man for some hundreds of years. As can easily be imagined it was an age crowded with many thrilling incidents while it also included much cruelty and futile strife; but when the results of the Viking rule are weighed it will be seen that the period produced much that was good and enduring.

The Norse reach the Irish Sea

The Norsemen appeared in the Irish Sea during the later part of the eighth century and began plundering the coasts of Ireland and Man. They particularly sought the churches and monasteries for they had scant respect for Christianity, while they knew that such places usually yielded rich spoil. The fear that the Norsemen inspired is shown by the following translation of a Gaelic verse written by an Irish scribe. Seated in his little hut near the sea, he is glad that a terrible storm is raging because it will prevent the pirates from approaching the shore:—

'The wind is boisterous to-night;
the white hair of the ocean is tousled.
I do not fear that there may come across the
Irish sea hordes of fierce Vikings.'*

*Porter, A. K., *The Crosses and Culture of Ireland*, New Haven, 1935, p. 75.

The earliest literary record of Viking raids in this part of the Irish Sea is that contained in the *Annals of Ulster* for the year A.D. 798 when there is the following entry—'*The burning of Inis Patrick by the heathen, and plunder taken from the districts; and the shrine of Dochonna was broken into by them, and great devastations on their part between Eire and Alba.*' It has formerly been assumed that the *Inis Patrick* (or *Inis Padraig* in the Gaelic) referred to was the Manx St. Patrick's Isle, on which the ruins of Peel Castle stand, but modern opinion favours its identification with Inispatrick, or St. Patrick's Isle in the Skerries off the Dublin coast. The nature of Dochonna's (or St. Conna's) shrine is not definitely indicated, but quite possibly it was a stone tomb built in the form of a small chapel. This is more likely than a former suggestion that the shrine was a small metal casket such as the one now preserved in the Museum at Copenhagen.*

For two centuries after 798 there is very little definite record of events in Man, although rather more is known of what was happening in surrounding lands, especially eastern Ireland. It is evident in any case that its important strategic position must have made Man a vitally significant base of operations for the Norsemen. In support of this it is frequently stated in one of the sagas—the *Orkneyinger's Saga*—that the Vikings would set off from the Island in the spring or early summer to raid the adjoining coasts, after which they would 'fare home to Man' in the autumn, before the winter storms began.

The effective occupation of Man, following the period of pirate expeditions, seems to date to the second half of the ninth century when the new masters seized the most fertile districts for their own use. The northern lowland still bears impressive evidence of this process in the form of a number of circular earthen mounds which probably mark the burial places of the more important farmer-warriors belonging to the first generation of Norse settlers. Such, at any rate, is the conclusion suggested as the result of careful excavations of typical mounds at Knoc y Doonee, Andreas, in 1927, as well as Ballateare, Jurby, in 1946, and supported by chance finds from others.

*While there is no clue as to the precise origin of this casket it was in all probability stolen from Ireland where the greater part of such metal-work was produced. It is definitely claimed to be of Irish origin by Dr. A. Mahr in his *Christian Art in Ancient Ireland*, I, Plates 16 and 17, Dublin, 1932; II, (1941), 109.

The Ballateare mound was forty-five feet in diameter and seven feet high, and in the centre was the body of the Viking warrior within a wooden coffin. In accordance with the pagan beliefs of the period, the man's armour including spears, sword and shield had been buried with him, after being broken in order to prevent the robbing of the grave. As a sacrifice to the dead man, the grave also contained, in addition to the body of a young person (possibly female), the bones of oxen, horses, sheep and dogs—these symbolising the live stock of the farmer-warrior, just as the sods of the mound bear witness to the fertile soil of the fields.

The Kingdom of Man and the Isles

Meanwhile, Scandinavian conquests and settlements took place around the coasts of Ireland, where Dublin was the centre of Norse power, as well as along the whole of western Scotland, and parts of north-west England and Wales. All districts conquered by the Norse were claimed by the king of Norway as being under his control, but in actual practice powerful Viking chieftains fought each other for supremacy. Thus at one time Man might be ruled by a king who lived in Dublin, at another time by a king who lived in the Island itself. There were other occasions when the Earls of Orkney claimed to rule the Island, especially during the eleventh century.

As time passed on, Man came to be linked particularly with the other Norse islands of the Hebrides along the west coast of Scotland, and the whole domain was called the Kingdom of Man and the Isles. There are in fact several hundred islands in the area if each islet is counted separately, but officially they were together reckoned as thirty-two in the days of the Kingdom, Man being the most important of all.

For the purposes of administration the Hebrides were divided into four groups, based on the main islands of Lewis, Skye, Mull and Islay. (See map, Fig. 24). These were further sub-divided into two groups, a northern and a southern, by the promontory of Ardnamurchan Point; and a fact of much interest which may be noted here is that the North Isles, namely, Lewis and Skye, were regarded as the Out Isles. The significance of this will become apparent in the next chapter when the origin of the Keys is discussed.

Godred Crovan (King Orry) (1079-1095)

With this king, who obtained the Manx throne in 1079, the history of the Island assumes a more continuous pattern, still, it is true, somewhat faint or blurred, instead of being the mere collection of unrelated scraps that it had previously been. But while Godred is the first king about whom anything very definite is known it must be admitted that much concerning him is very obscure. His nickname, Crovan, is supposed to be due to the fact that he always wore white gauntlets when he went to war. Godred's home was possibly Islay, though he is said to have spent part of his youth in Man. He fought with the Norwegians under Harold, King of Norway, against Harold of England at Stamford Bridge in 1066, and, following on the English victory, Godred fled to Man. Nothing is heard of him for some years, but he then appears on the scene as the leader of three expeditions against Man, having somehow gathered together an army and a fleet. His first two attacks were unsuccessful, but in 1079 he made an attack which gave him possession of the Island.

The way in which he succeeded in this final attempt is described in the *Chronicle of Man and the Isles*, compiled later on by the monks of Rushen Abbey. Godred landed at Ramsey during the night, and hid three hundred men on the slopes of Scacafell, now called Skyhill. At daybreak the Manx fiercely attacked the invaders, but during the heat of the fray, the three hundred men in ambush attacked the natives in the rear. Disheartened, the Manx attempted to flee; but the tide was in flood, and as it came further up the Sulby river then than it does now, they were cut off on all sides. They piteously begged Godred to spare their lives, as he had been reared amongst them, and he, taking compassion on them, forbade his army to attack them further. Thus Godred became King of Man and reigned for sixteen years; and except for short intervals his descendants ruled it until 1265. This great warrior can hardly have spent much time in the Island, since his dominions included Dublin, where he resided a great deal, in addition to the Western Isles of Scotland. It was in the island of Islay that he died in 1095.

Godred was the ruler who was responsible for the union of Man and the Isles into one kingdom; and to administer this

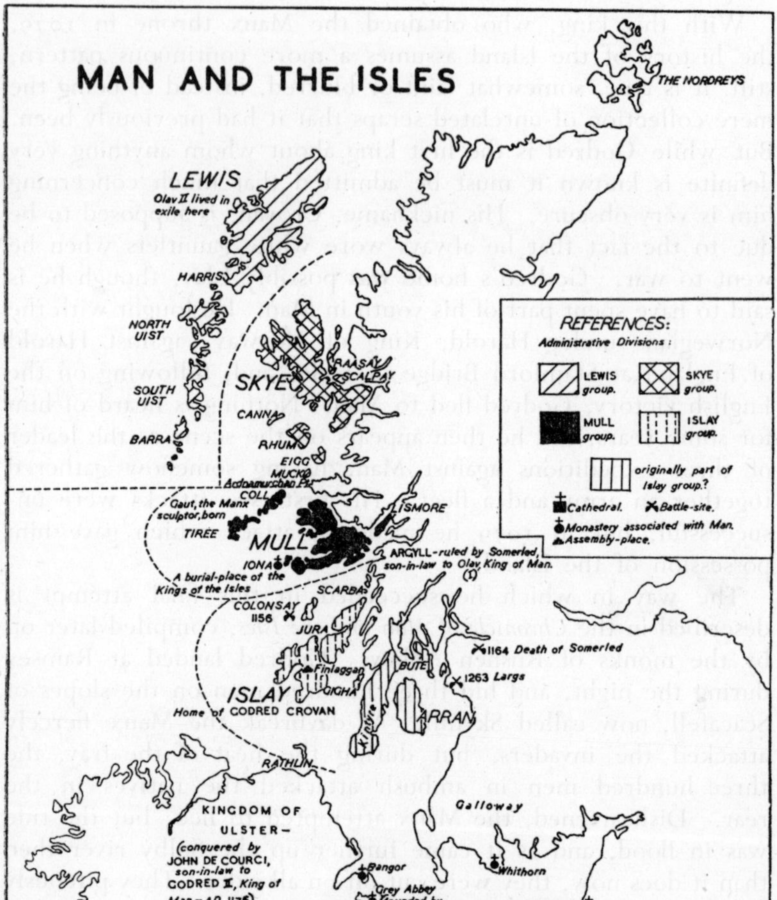

Fig. 24.—The Kingdom of Man and the Isles

great maritime unit he devised an ingenious political system which will be discussed in the next chapter. True, as will be seen, his great plan fell to pieces in less than two centuries after its creation, but there is reason to believe that in one respect at least, that is, as regards the number of the Keys, his system had a very important bearing on subsequent developments.

The Gaelic form of Godred was Gorry, which lost its initial 'G,' after the title, king, to produce the more familiar name Orry. Tradition says that when he first came to Man, he landed at the Lhen on a bright starry night. Those who were gathered on the shore asked him whence he had come, and, pointing upwards to the Milky Way he said, 'Yonder is the road whence I came, and along that star-spangled dome is the way that leads to my country.' Ever since that time the Milky Way has been called in Manx, *Raad Mooar Ree Gorry*, or 'the Great Way of King Orry.' This picturesque legend shows what a great national hero Godred had become in the imagination of the people.

King Magnus of Norway Visits Man (1098-1103)

After the death of Godred Crovan came a period of conflict in which the two divisions of the Island, the North and the South, fought against one another. In 1098 a conflict took place which is referred to in the *Chronicle of Man*. According to the story there were two rival chieftains, Ottar and Macmarus, about whom nothing else is known. In their struggle for supremacy a great battle took place at a ford called Santwat which is thought to have been near Peel. According to tradition the North gained victory owing to the assistance of their women, but the leaders of both sides perished in the struggle.

Just after this battle, Magnus Barefoot, King of Norway, came to assert his supremacy over the various Norse conquests. In 1098 he arrived at St. Patrick's Isle with a fleet of 160 ships, and he was so pleased with the Island's fertility that he chose it as his chief residence. Like other ambitious monarchs, he conquered as much as possible of other lands around the Irish Sea. After humbling the men of Galloway, who were compelled to supply timber for the erection of three forts on the Island, he set off to subdue Anglesey. Next he turned his attention to Ireland, where he lost his life in 1103.

King Olaf I (1113-1153)

After the death of Magnus there was apparently another period of confusion until the accession of Olaf I, probably in the year 1113. He was the youngest son of Godred Crovan, and had lived at the English court of Henry I since his father's death. His long reign of about forty years was one of the most memorable in the Island's history. Described in the *Chronicle* as a man of peace he showed such wisdom and skill, and kept on such friendly terms with the rulers of England, as well as those of Ireland and Scotland, that no one ventured to disturb his own Kingdom of Man and the Isles until he had grown old and feeble. During his reign the foundation of the Cistercian monastery at Rushen Abbey took place, Olaf having granted the site to the Abbot of Furness. Tragedy marked the end of Olaf's reign since he was treacherously murdered by his nephews who came over from Dublin to demand a share of his kingdom.

Godred II (1153-1187)

Olaf's son Godred was in Norway doing homage to the Norwegian king on behalf of his father at the time of the latter's death. Returning immediately to Man he dealt sternly with Olaf's murderers. Shortly afterwards he set sail for Dublin with a number of ships and a large army since he had been offered the throne of the Scandinavian kingdom there. Despite stiff opposition, Godred obtained possession of Dublin and then returned to Man. Here, he so offended the chiefs of the Isles who had helped him on this Irish expedition, that they rebelled against him with the aid of his brother-in-law, Somerled, the ruler of the Scottish coast of Argyll, who was of Norwegian extraction as his name indicates. In 1156 Godred was defeated in a great naval battle off Colonsay, and was forced to share the Kingdom of Man and the Isles with Somerled. The latter took the islands of Mull and Islay off the coast of Argyll, which formed the southernmost of the Hebrides, while Godred retained Man and the northern group of Lewis and Skye. As a result of this curious arrangement the hold of the Manx kings on their other island possessions was permanently weakened, although they retained the title of King of the Isles. The monks of Rushen Abbey, mournfully recording these events in the *Chronicle of Man*, wrote ' thus was the Kingdom of the Isles ruined from the time the sons of Somerled got possession of it.' Godred seems to have felt his throne in danger since, after his struggle with Somerled in 1156, he put himself under the protection of Henry II of England.

Godred and Somerled quarrelled again in 1158 when the latter appeared off Ramsey with a fleet of fifty-three ships. He drove Godred out of the Island and then plundered the area before retiring to Scotland. In 1164 Somerled was slain in an attack against Scotland. Meanwhile, Godred, who had gone to Norway to seek assistance returned to resume possession of his Island kingdom. He ultimately died in 1187; and it is significant that, although he died in Man, his body was carried next year to Iona, the island made holy by the work of St. Columba.

Reginald I (1187-1228)

Godred left three sons, Reginald, Olaf, and Ivar, and while Reginald was the eldest he was not strictly the heir to the throne, since he had been born many years before the marriage of his parents. The lawful heir was Olaf, and he was supposed to succeed; but as he was then only ten years old, the nobles preferred his older brother as their king. Reginald, who thus succeeded his father, stood out as one of the most warlike princes of his age, having spent much of his time in the manner of the ancient sea-kings. In proof of this, one of the sagas declares that he had passed three successive years always on board his ship, never being for one single hour beneath the roof of a house! Just where he performed his exploits is not quite clear, but probably most of them were in northern Scotland and the Orkneys.

As King of Man he had to face many troubles, most of which were due to the inevitable quarrels between his brother Olaf and himself and their various supporters. The details of such quarrels are wearying so that we need only concern ourselves with the main incidents. To begin with, Reginald gave his brother Olaf the island of Lewis, one of the northern Hebrides. Despite its size it was much poorer than Man, since it consisted mainly of moorland, and its inhabitants lived chiefly by hunting and fishing. Olaf therefore complained that he was unable to support himself and his retinue on such a poor island and asked for a larger share of the dominions. Reginald's reply was to have his brother imprisoned in Scotland. In the end Olaf escaped: and in 1224 he gathered a fleet of thirty-two ships from the Isles and came to Man, landing at Ronaldsway. Reginald now gave his brother many more islands, but kept Man for himself. Neither was satisfied and so Man was again plunged into civil war. The North was on the side of Olaf, while the South supported Reginald. The opposing forces met in 1228 at Tynwald Hill, where Reginald was slain and his followers routed. The unfortunate Southerners had a very unhappy time on this occasion, for not only did they lose the battle, but just afterwards their land was visited by pirates, and the area was devastated!

Apart from all these squabbles Reginald's stormy reign has one other feature of significance, namely, that it showed the increasing power of the English king in the Irish Sea, with the correspondingly waning power of the Norwegian king. Like previous ambitious rulers, Reginald could not resist the temptation to interfere in Irish affairs, particularly in northern Ireland. This considerably annoyed the English King John, because England was anxious to extend her own power in Ireland, since the previous king, Henry II, had assumed the title of Lord of Ireland in 1171 when he added to his possessions by annexing Dublin and some other ports. Hence Reginald was sharply summoned to appear before the English king in 1206 and to do homage to him.

The king of Norway was also trying to assert his former authority over the Manx ruler, and indeed Reginald set off to Norway to do homage there. This so irritated John of England that in 1210 he sent an expedition against the Isle of Man while its king was away, and, on his return, Reginald had to appear before John once again. Reginald's career as a monarch can thus hardly be described as a happy one!

Olaf II (1228-1237)

After the death of his brother in 1228, Olaf gained possession of Man, although he was not able to regain all the other isles

Fig. 25.—Silver ornaments of the Viking period found in Man. The larger torc and the small armlet were found at Ballacamaish, Andreas; the half torc formed part of the famous Douglas treasure trove in 1894

Fig. 26.—St. German's Cathedral

that had formerly belonged to the kingdom. Since he had received some help from Norway, the English king, now Henry III, showed his annoyance by bringing Olaf before him and making him promise to defend the Irish Sea against intruders, and if necessary, to place fifty ships at the disposal of England. This naturally displeased the Norwegians, and Olaf was on the point of setting out for Norway to try and make his peace there when he died.

Harald I (1237-1248)

Olaf II's son Harald was only fourteen when he succeeded his father, and his reign witnessed still more rivalry between England and Norway for the control of Man and the Isles. At first Harald refused to recognise the Norwegian monarch as his overlord, with the result that he was deposed, and the revenues of the country were collected by King Haakon of Norway. In the end Harald submitted, and received back his kingdom which gave him a friendly welcome. Then the English ruler, Henry III, showed his favour by knighting him, but this, of course, aroused the jealousy of Norway. Once more Harald set off to the latter country where he received such a warm reception that he married King Haakon's daughter. Tragedy befell him on his return journey, for he and his queen were shipwrecked and drowned near the Shetlands. His brother succeeded to the throne as Reginald II, but his reign was only to last a few weeks since he was assassinated by one of his knights, Ivar, in a meadow near Rushen Church.

King Magnus (1252-1265)

A period of confusion and strife followed the tragic death of Reginald II, but finally in 1252 Magnus, youngest son of Olaf II, secured the Manx throne, and he was fated to be the last king of Man and the Isles. It has already been seen that England and Norway were competing for the control of Man. Meanwhile Scotland had been growing in strength, and its king, Alexander III, was anxious to obtain possession of the Western Isles. By this time only some of these islands (Lewis and Skye with their 'pertinents') belonged to Man, the others being in the hands of the descendants of Somerled.

After vainly trying to get them by bargaining, Alexander attacked the Hebrides. King Haakon of Norway arrived off the Scottish coast with a large fleet to defend the islands, but in 1263 he suffered a reverse at the battle of Largs, on the Firth of Clyde. Meanwhile the Manx king, Magnus, had also taken a fleet to oppose the Scots, but he was not present at the battle of Largs, having proceeded up Loch Long to attack that coast. Upon the retreat of the Norwegians, Magnus returned to Man with Alexander in pursuit. After a truce the two kings met in Dumfries, where Magnus was allowed to keep the Isle of Man after doing homage to King Alexander, and promising to supply him with ten war-galleys—five 24-oared, and five 12-oared—whenever he needed them. Thus for the last two years of his life Magnus was king of Man only; and he was the last of the dynasty founded by Godred Crovan to hold that position, since in 1266, a year after the death of Magnus, a treaty was signed between Norway and Scotland, in which not only the Western Isles of Scotland, but also Man, were handed over to the king of Scotland.

REFERENCES

KENDRICK, T. D., *A History of the Vikings*, London, 1929.
SHETELIG, H. and FALK, H., *Scandinavian Archaeology*, Oxford, 1937.
MARSTRANDER, C. J. S., *Norse Conquest of the Isle of Man*, Oslo, 1932.
MOORE, A. W., *History of the Isle of Man*, I, 82-177, London, 1900.
The Chronicle of Man and the Sudreys, with historical notes by P. A. Munch, 2 vols., Manx Society, Douglas, 1874.
The Orkneyinger's Saga, vol. III of Icelandic Sagas, London, 1894.
KERMODE, P. M. C., Peel Island and the Shrine of St. Mochonna, *Proc. I.M. Nat. Hist. and Antiq. Soc.*, I, 585-591, Douglas, 1914.
The Shrine of Dachonna and Peel Islet, *Journal of the Manx Museum*, III, 1935.
ANDERSON, A. O., *Early Sources of Scottish History*, A.D. *500-1286*, 2 vols. Edinburgh, 1922.
MEGAW, B. R. S., St. Patrick's Isle: The Tara of the Isle of Man, *Journal of the Manx Museum*, V, 1943.

Chapter V.

DEVELOPMENTS DURING THE SCANDINAVIAN PERIOD

We are inclined to think of the Norse sea-rovers as ruthless and cruel, with an insatiable passion for warfare and plunder. It is true that, at first, they were enemies of Christianity; but they were a fine virile people with a great love of freedom, and they gave life and vigour to the regions in which they settled. They were not barbarians. They had the art of writing, and a great appreciation of beauty, as they showed in their love of ornaments (Fig. 25) and fine clothing, and in the decoration of their wonderful carvings in stone and wood. Their weapons show their skill in working iron, as their clothing, often with very graceful patterns, shows their skill in weaving. They were practical resourceful men, and great organisers. In this connection the essential thing to remember is that when they entered a country with old and settled traditions, such as Man at that period, they came under the influence of the local culture and devoted their skill and power of organisation to developing and improving what they found.

In their physical make-up, as already seen in Chapter I, the Vikings are thought to have been mainly fair, tall and long-headed, belonging to what is called the Nordic race type; and there are many people of this kind in Man at the present day as a result of the Norse invasions. As previously explained, there are rather more people of this type in the parishes of the northern lowland and in the parish of Malew than elsewhere, partly because these areas contain so much of the richer agricultural land. It should also be remembered that these parts offered the best low-lying shores on which the shallow and flat-bottomed boats could be pulled up when they came to stay for the winter or for longer periods, so that they were the most attractive areas for the Norsemen.

Generally speaking, it was only the younger men who came from Norway, possibly bringing with them a few slaves. Thus, from the beginning, there must have been constant intermixture between the Norsemen and the native women inhabitants of the Island, so that there would soon be a fusion of the two elements to form a new Manx type. Since the Vikings were known to the Gaels as ' Strangers ' (Galls) the mixed population of Man came to be called the Gael-Galls by the other Gaelic people in districts unaffected by Scandinavian immigration.

Manx and Norse Languages

The Norse language was naturally introduced into Man; and since it was the language of the conquerors it came to be the speech used by the upper classes and also in the government of the country. Gaelic must also have been used by the women, who would teach it to the children. When the Kingdom of Man and the Isles came to an end, the Norse language gradually died away, and the Celtic tongue once more became the chief speech of the Manx. Owing to the close connection that had existed between Man and Scotland, particularly the south-west and the Western Isles, the native tongue of Man had become strongly influenced by the Scottish form of Gaelic, so that henceforth Manx had a somewhat greater resemblance to Scottish Gaelic than to Irish. Surprising as it may seem, the Norse language had scarcely any effect on modern Manx.

Norse Place-Names

Survivals of the Norse occupation still persist in many places ending in *by*, which was a Scandinavian word for farm or homestead, so that Sulby originally meant Solli's farm, Colby meant Colli's farm, and so on. The Scandinavian word for mountain was *fell*, and thus Snaefell is pure Norse for snow-mountain. The Norse name *dalr*, meaning a dale or valley, is found in the names of many glens in the Island, as in Foxdale, meaning waterfall-dale, while Dalby means the farm in the dale or glen. Many names of places on the coast are also of Norse origin, although as the names are written now it is not always too easy to see this. Thus the Norse word *vik*, meaning creek, is now found in the form wick, as in the case of such bays as Fleshwick and Perwick.

This fascinating but complicated subject can be studied in more detail in the well-known books by A. W. Moore, and J. J. Kneen on the *Place Names of the Isle of Man*, which deal not only with Norse, but also with Celtic, and English place-names. (See also the Appendix, page 166, giving a glossary of Gaelic and Norse words most often found in Manx place-names).

Mode of Life—Buildings, Clothing, Food

Records dealing with the Isle of Man tell nothing of how the people lived here. There are, nevertheless, descriptions of life in Iceland and the Western Isles, and it may, perhaps, be assumed that the Vikings who settled in Man wore the same kind of dress and lived in the same kind of homes. Their houses were rather long and narrow, with low walls built of stones and earth, and a very steep roof covered with turf, straw, or rushes. The rooms had open hearths in the centre of the floor from which the smoke escaped through a hole in the roof, and the people slept on beds made of straw placed round the walls. The chiefs and prominent men lived on their own estates with their families, followers and servants. On such an estate there would be a dwelling-house and a series of farm buildings, the whole arranged so as to form a quadrangle. The buildings were all detached from one another, and often even the different parts of the dwelling-house—the kitchen, the dining-hall and so on—were under separate roofs, although, later on, people were able to erect larger houses with more rooms under one roof.

It appears to have been customary for more than one family to live in the same household, since the married son or sons, and in some cases the married daughters, remained on the farm with their families doing their share of the work. The result was to form large family units consisting of two or more generations, all under the strict control of the patriarch, or head of the whole group.

The men wore grey woollen trousers, kept in position by a belt, and often had the socks knitted on to them. They also wore a linen shirt or woollen tunic, a cloak, and shoes made of raw hides like the former Manx *carranes*, or sandals. The most important piece of women's clothing was the long gown, or *kyrtil*, made very wide, and fastened round the waist by a belt. They were very fond of ornaments. Brooches, finger-rings, and bracelets are often mentioned in the sagas, while rich finds of ornaments in silver and bronze have often been found in their graves. When they could obtain them, by plunder or other means, the Vikings loved fine clothes in many colours. One account of 968 speaks of the Norsemen in Limerick possessing ' woven cloths of every kind and colour, silk and satin raiment, beauteous and variegated, both scarlet and green.'

Their bread was made of rye, oats or barley, as little wheat was sown. In the summer, herrings would be plentiful, and there would be meat as well as milk, butter, and cheese from the cattle. Curds and whey seem to have been very popular. Judging by what happened in later times, many of the people would go into the mountain pastures, or *earys*, during the summer months, since good pastures for the animals would be found there, and turf could also be obtained for winter fuel. The problem of curing food for winter consumption must, on the other hand, have been difficult, since salt was scarce and had to be imported, unless it was obtained by boiling sea-water.

Trade

Trade appears to have been more important than it is usually thought. The Norseman with his great love for, and his great skill on, the sea could and did become a great trader when not engaged in some raiding enterprise. It is, indeed, known that active trading took place between Norway, through the various Norse settlements in the west, such as those in western Scotland and around the Irish Sea, with France and the countries of southern Europe. From the north came fish, hides, and furs, while to the north went woollen and linen cloths, as well as corn, honey, and wine. There was also a great trade in slaves who had been made prisoners in war. Just what part the Island played in all this traffic it is impossible to say at the moment, but there can be little doubt that the existence of these trading movements definitely contributed to the persistence of the Kingdom of Man and the Isles for some two centuries.

Government and Administration—The Tynwald Court

The Manx system of government illustrates very strikingly two things, firstly the influence of ideas introduced by the Norsemen, and secondly the genius of these people for turning to account customs which were in existence amongst the people they had conquered. An essential feature of the Norse life was the annual open-air assembly of all the freemen at some central place where new laws were announced, disputes settled, and other necessary business dealt with. This assembly was called the *thing*, a word which forms the first part of the Manx term Tynwald. The second half is Norse for field or meeting place, so that Tynwald (or *Thingwald*) was originally the place at which the assembly of freemen met. This is the meeting which is still held every Tynwald Day, July 5th, for the purpose of announcing new laws that have been passed during the preceding year; and until the war of 1914-1918 it was true to say that laws did not become effective until they had been approved at this ceremony.

As has been said, the mound called Tynwald Hill (Fig. 27) is much older than the Scandinavian period, and in all probability it was a burial mound of the Bronze Age. A national assembly, or fair, had been held long before the coming of the Norse on this site which is the natural meeting place for the whole Island. The date of the fair was originally Mid-summer Day, a day associated with much rejoicing from very early pagan times. With the coming of Christianity into the Island, the fair was linked with the name of a Christian saint, John the Baptist, whose place in the church's calendar, June 24th, was as near as possible to mid-summer's day. Then, with the alteration of the calendar that took place in the eighteenth century, the date was changed to July 5th, the present date of the Tynwald ceremony and fair. Further, although the name, Tynwald Hill, is the name by which the mound is generally known, the Celtic name by which it is still known locally is *Cronk y Keeillown*, i.e., the Hill of St. John's Chapel, or Keeill.

Nowadays, the Lieutenant-Governor takes the central seat on Tynwald Hill, the seat once occupied by the Norse king. With him is the Bishop, the successor to the chief priest of the pagan temple of Thor. In front are the Deemsters and the members of the Legislative Council, who were formerly the Lord's principal officers. On the next platform are the twenty-four members of the Keys; below these are the Vicars and the Captains of the parishes, and outside the mound are the Freemen or Commons.

The Deemsters

The position which the Deemsters hold in the Tynwald ceremony is, historically, the most important part of their

Fig. 27.—St. John's Fair and Tynwald, about 1850
(Note the canvas pavilion erected over Tynwald Hill, which is a very old feature)

office. It has already been explained why there are two; they represent the two original main divisions of the Island, the North and South. It has also been seen how their name has changed from the Celtic *briw*, meaning judge, and the Norse *lagman*, meaning man of the law, to the English *deemster*, meaning the man who 'steers' or guides the 'doom' or judgment.

For a long time the laws were not written, and were supposed to be locked in the memories, or the 'breasts,' of the men appointed for that purpose. It was the duty of the law-men to declare to the king what the laws were. Such declarations were called 'breast-laws,' and they were, of course, based on the general customs of the Island. These form the basis of the existing Manx customary or common law, but they remained oral until about 1690 despite various attempts to have them committed to writing. It was then that Deemster Parr wrote his *Abstract of the Laws, Customs and Ordinances of the Isle of Man* which did a great deal towards making Manx common law more stable and reliable, and less dependent on the memories or caprices of the Deemsters.

The Keys

The Manx House of Keys, which now corresponds to the English House of Commons, owes some of its characteristic features to the Norse period, including the fixing of its number which still remains at twenty-four. The earliest Keys were those chosen from the chief landowners as being 'the worthiest man in the land' to represent the freemen of the Island, whose duty it was to assist at Tynwald in deciding what the law was. It was not until a later period that their function came to include the making of new laws.

Meanwhile how did such a number arise? A very possible explanation is to be found in a consideration of the system created by Godred Crovan—the King Orry of Manx tradition—to govern his maritime Kingdom of Man and the Isles. As pointed out in the previous chapter, it was assumed that the area consisted of thirty-two islands, and it was decided that the common parliament should comprise the same number of chosen representatives. Of these thirty-two members, Man, being the wealthiest island and the capital, was to appoint one half. The other sixteen came from the Hebrides, which were divided into the four groups of isles already described, each group sending four representatives to the Tynwald Court.

The next stage came after the partition of the Isles, dating from Somerled's defeat of Godred II in 1156, as a result of which only the two northern groups, or Out Isles, maintained their connection with Man. This reduced the Hebridean membership to eight, and gave a total of twenty-four Keys, a number which was destined to remain permanent.

In 1266, at the time of the break-up of the Kingdom, and the cession of all the Western Isles to the crown of Scotland, only the sixteen Manxmen were left in the Keys. But the Manx refused to accept their defeat as final, and they continued to fill the places formerly occupied by the men from the Out Isles by appointing eight additional representatives from Man itself—thus preserving the total which has persisted to the present day.

Keeping these points in mind it is not difficult to interpret the statement made by the Keys themselves in their famous declaration regarding the Manx constitution in 1422. Explaining the origin of the number to Sir John Stanley they said that the Keys 'were twenty-four freeholders, namely eight in the Out Isles and sixteen in your land of Mann—and that was in King Orry's days.' Until recently the term Out Isles in this statement was taken to mean the whole of the Hebridean group, but such an interpretation is now seen to be incorrect.

An arresting feature concerning the original representation in Man is that it was probably on a parish basis, for there is no doubt that there were sixteen ancient parishes in early days when Marown was joined to Santan, and not seventeen as at present. When, in the end, the additional eight members had to be chosen from within the Island, the parochial basis of the Keys was upset, and the sheadings came to be adopted as the units of representation.

The origin of the name Keys has given rise to a good deal of discussion and it cannot be said that the problem is finally solved. The suggested derivation from a Scandinavian word *kjosa* meaning 'chosen' cannot be accepted on linguistic grounds; but the most likely explanation is that it is an English word which owes its introduction to the following combination of circumstances. In the first place, the Manx name for the Keys has long been *Yn Kiare-as-feed*, literally meaning 'The Four and twenty.' Such a title would, no doubt, be more or less unintelligible to the earliest English officials who came to the Island, but they probably saw some resemblance in pronunciation between the first words 'kiare-as' and 'keys.' Then, since the essential function of the body in its original form was to 'unlock' or solve the difficulties of the law, it seemed quite apt and convenient for the English to use the term keys in its figurative sense to describe its members. This word is, indeed, used in its Latin form of *claves* in the earliest document in the Statute Book dated 1418, in which the Keys are described as *Claves Manniae et Claves Legis* (i.e. 'Keys of Man and Keys of the Law'). The term Keys is not found in documents between 1418 and 1585, but between 1585 and 1734 the title 'the 24 Keys' is used; and from 1734 onwards the phrase is 'the Keys.'

Fencing the Court

Before the Tynwald ceremony begins, the Court is 'fenced.' That is to say, the chief coroner, the coroner of Glenfaba sheading, reads out a notice in which all are warned not to 'quarrel, brawl or make any disturbance.' We read in accounts of Norse assemblies of an actual fence made of sacred cords or ropes being drawn around the place where the Court sat. 'Fencing the court' is thus a Norse institution. But the practice of strewing the pathway from St. John's Church to Tynwald Hill with rushes goes back to pagan days in the Island when Manannan, the Celtic sea-god, received rushes as his annual tribute.

Some Tynwald promulgation ceremonies have been held at places other than St. John's. It is recorded that a Tynwald was held at Cronk Urleigh, Kirk Michael, in 1422, and at Cronk Keeill Abban, Kirk Braddan, a few years later.

Administrative Divisions

It has already been shown that the original division into sheadings, parishes, treens and quarterlands was not the work of the Norse, but that the Norsemen caused them to be better defined and more fully organised. Each sheading is believed to have had the duty of supplying one war-galley for the Island's defence, while each of the treens had to supply four men to serve in this ship. Later on, the obligation of the landholders to supply ships and men was altered to an obligation to pay taxes to the king. A charter dating to the year 1313, by which the king of Scotland handed over the Isle of Man to the Earl of Moray, makes it a condition that the Earl should annually place six ships, each with twenty-six oars, at the disposal of the Scottish king, and this may possibly be merely a revival of what the Norse kings of Man had demanded from the Island.

Religion During the Scandinavian Period

With the coming of the pagan Norsemen, the development of Christianity was seriously checked for at least a century. It was not until about the middle of the tenth century that there was a marked revival of Christianity, and the Norse began to give up their pagan beliefs. Their conversion appears to have been a very slow process, and even after they had adopted some forms of the Christian religion they still loved to think of the stories connected with their old gods and heroes, since many of these are recorded, as will be seen later, on what were intended as Christian memorial crosses.

An interesting discovery from the period when the Norse were still pagan was made in 1927, when a grave which possibly dates to as early as the mid-ninth century was excavated. This had the form of a low mound, seven or eight feet high, situated on a hill overlooking the Ayre at Knoc y Doonee, in the parish of Andreas. It proved to be a ship-burial, for the local landowner had been placed in his own boat, which was about 30 feet long, the whole being then covered with earth. In the boat were also placed his sword, spear, shield and battle-axe, while his fishing-gear, and his hammer and tongs were added. Finally, his horse and dog were sacrificed so that they might accompany their master in his journey to the next world. Few ornaments were found in the grave, but it is significant that a small bronze brooch of Irish type was discovered, and this had no doubt been made by some Celtic worker. More recently a similar boat-burial has been found at Balladoole (Arbory) in the Castletown lowland, while as previously noted (p. 50) another type of Viking grave was excavated in the north at Ballateare in 1946.

When first converted to Christianity the Manx Vikings adopted the Celtic mode of organisation in which there were no such institutions as dioceses, nor bishops with territorial jurisdiction. But in all likelihood during the early half of the eleventh century they began to break their links with the Irish church at about the time when Iceland and Orkney also came under Roman influence direct from Continental Europe, and the first bishop of Man, who bore the ancient Norse name Roolwer (which is the same as our Rollo or Ralph) dates to the middle of the eleventh century. Doubtless he owed allegiance to the English Primate, the Archbishop of Canterbury, and it is very likely that Roolwer's successor, Bishop William, was a Norman monk.

The Development of Rushen Abbey

No definite information about the further development of the Christian church is available until the time of King Olaf, (1113-1153) who, having been educated at the English court, must have been familiar with the English religious system. In all probability it was during his reign that the Island was organised into parishes, each with its recognised parish church or Kirk, and it is definitely known that in 1134 Olaf invited the monks of Furness to come and found Rushen Abbey.

The monks of Furness belonged to a Roman Catholic order known as the Cistercian, which stressed the importance of doing manual work as well as performing the ordinary religious duties. They took a great interest in the improvement of agriculture and the breeding of animals, and no doubt the brethren at Rushen Abbey helped to improve methods of farming among the Manx people. The neighbourhood of Rushen Abbey must have been very marshy in those days, and it certainly involved a great deal of hard labour to lay firm foundations for the group of stone buildings whose ruins still remain there.

The Abbey became a centre of great importance and many roads led to it. It was in close touch with the great landing place at Ronaldsway (now called Derbyhaven), while routes connected it through Foxdale with St. John's and so to Peel. A very important road led by way of St. Mark's and the Braaid, on by the old church of Marown, across the central valley, thence following the mountain road to Ramsey, another very important landing place. The growing significance of the Abbey may be judged from the fact that a number of the Norse kings were buried there, including Olaf II, Reginald II and Magnus, the last King of Man and the Isles.

At the outset Rushen Abbey was granted considerable tracts of land in Malew, and as time went on it became still more wealthy. Olaf I's son, Godred, gave lands in Lezayre for the building of another abbey there, but these soon passed into the hands of Rushen Abbey. In 1246, under King Harald, the monks obtained the use of 'all kinds of mines' in Man, as well as some land near St. Trinian's, and they were granted exemption from all tolls and taxes. Thus the power of the Abbey became very great indeed, and with it grew the influence of the Pope in the affairs of the Island.

The Bishopric of Sodor and Man

King Olaf I strengthened the links between Man and the Isles and organised its religious activities by spreading Roman Catholic forms of ritual and administration against the opposition of Irish monks who continued to assert their authority at Iona as late as 1203. This work was actually entrusted to the monks of Furness Abbey to whom was granted, in 1134, the right of electing the bishops of the Isles. The correct title of the diocese is *Ecclesia Insularum* (i.e. the Episcopal See of the Isles), or *Ecclesia Sodorensis*—the latter being the Latin form of the Norse name for Man and the Hebrides, the *Sudreyjar* (Sudreys), or 'Southern Isles.' They were so called to distinguish them from the Nordreys, or Northern Isles, including the Shetlands and Orkneys.

Although the political connections between Man and the Isles ceased after 1266, the religious link persisted until about the fifteenth century. At the present day there is no connection at all, but the title of the Manx bishop serves as a reminder of Norse days. Strictly the actual title now used—Sodor and Man—is rather superfluous, but it came into use during the seventeenth century when the original meaning of the term Sodorensis was not fully appreciated. From 1152 until the fifteenth century the bishopric was under the control of the archbishop of Trondhjem in Norway, but now it forms part of the English province of York, an act of 1542 having confirmed the transference which had been made almost a century earlier.

Bishop Simon

The best known bishop of Sodor and Man during the Norse period was Simon, who held office from 1227 until about 1247. According to the *Chronicle of Man* he was a man 'of great prudence, and learned in the Holy Scriptures.' It was he, who, according to the *Chronicle*, began to build St. German's on Peel islet as the Cathedral Church of the Sudreys about the year 1230. When he became bishop there were very likely two churches on that small island, a spot of very special sacredness. One of the churches was St. Patrick's (an eleventh or early twelfth century building, now in ruins, but originally the parish church of Kirk Patrick) while the other was presumably the ancient parish church of Kirk German on the site now occupied by the ruins of the Cathedral. Simon selected St. German's not only because of its association with the traditional first Bishop of the Celtic Church in Man, but possibly because it had a larger endowment of land, and proceeded to rebuild it. He did not complete the work being able only to finish the chancel, and also the tower and transepts, while the nave was built some years later by Bishop Richard. Simon was buried in his own Cathedral which continued to be used until the middle of the eighteenth century, but has since become dilapidated (Fig. 26). He is said to have had his palace in Kirk Michael on the site of the existing Bishopscourt, but apart from the tower the present building belongs to a later date.

Stone Crosses of the Scandinavian Period: Their Characteristics

It has been seen in Chapter III that the art of carving on stone had already made great strides among the Manx before the Norsemen arrived, and that the form of memorial known as the Celtic cross had been developed by them. Native Celtic sculptors still went on with their art after the Norse conquest, thus indicating that they must have retained their Christian beliefs; and indeed they then produced very refined examples of Celtic crosses which do not show any traces of Scandinavian influence. When the Norse settlers adopted Christianity and began to erect monuments to their dead, they naturally copied the models with which they were familiar, either in Man or in the Hebrides. Thus a new series of crosses—the Scandinavian—began from at least the middle of the tenth century, and these reveal certain differences from those previously made in Man.

In the first place, the language of the inscriptions is Norse and the lettering is a special script known as Runic. These Runes represent the oldest form of writing among the Teutonic peoples, including the Scandinavian, and appear to be based mainly on the Roman letters, simplified so that they could be carved more easily on stone or on wood. It will be seen by the illustration (Fig. 28) that they consist almost entirely of straight lines since it is most difficult to cut on stone or wood.

The inscriptions are not very long, but say something like this:—' Joalf son of Thorolf the Red erected this cross to the memory of Fritha his mother.' Some of the inscriptions are nevertheless very significant since they give actual proof of the mixing of Norse with Celtic people. For example, on one stone, a man with a Norse name, Thorleif, refers to his son who had a Celtic name, Fiac, and no doubt the mother was also Celtic. Other people named on the stones had purely Celtic names (e.g. Mael Brigde, and Druian, son of Dugald) yet their memorials were written in Norse!

The makers of the Scandinavian crosses added fresh details to the decorations, and also depicted new subjects. As an actual example of one new design reference might be made to the work of the earliest and best known of Scandinavian sculptors named Gaut, who came from the island of Coll, and who was responsible for the ' twist-and-ring ' pattern so well shown in the crosses known as Gaut's Cross, Michael, Thor's Cross, Bride, or the Sandulf Cross, Andreas. As time passed on, the Norse craftsmen broke away from the rather stiff designs of the earlier Celtic workers and became bolder in introducing more and more figures of animals, including the typical dragons, and human beings into their work.

This leads to what is probably the most fascinating aspect of all, namely, the way in which the crosses were used to illustrate stories of the doings of pagan gods, particularly Odin, father of the gods, of the giant Hymi, with whom Thor once went fishing, or Rungnir, who challenged the great god to mortal

Fig. 28.—Runic letters (first two lines) carved on stone at Kirk Maughold. The lowest line illustrates Ogham characters for the letters, B, L, F (V), S, N, H, D, T, C, Q.

Fig. 28a.—Folk Museum, Cregneash

combat. There were also stories of human heroes, the favourite of whom was Sigurd who slew the dragon Fafni and carried off his hoard of gold. The Norsemen must have taken a keen delight in reciting such stirring deeds during the long winter nights, and these stories remained vividly in their memories long after their adoption of Christianity. They could not resist carving many scenes from such exploits on their stone memorials, along with symbols and stories derived from Christian sources. Thus the Scandinavian crosses represent a striking mixture of pagan and Christian beliefs.

Fig. 29 shows fragments of the broken crosses from Jurby and Malew, dating from about the end of the tenth century, by different artists, but both recording portions of the famous Sigurd story. Sigurd had been advised by Odin to dig a pit in which to conceal himself so that he might pierce the dragon, Fafni, with his famous sword, as the monster passed over. Both crosses illustrate this incident on their right-hand panels, and the monster is seen writhing in its death-agony. Above this, on the Malew cross, Sigurd is shown roasting ring-shaped portions of the dragon's heart, held on a spit over a fire, which is depicted by three triangular tongues of flame. Having scalded his fingers with boiling blood he cools them in his mouth; and, once the blood touches his tongue, he understands the language of the birds (one of which is shown near the bottom of the Jurby stone), who tell him of the treachery being planned by a dwarf, Regin. The same part of the story is represented on the Jurby cross below the dragon, but the picture is much less clear. Sigurd's horse, Grani, is also shown on the upper left-hand panel of the Malew cross (only the fore portion of the animal having been preserved), while the horse also figures on the Jurby cross. Other incidents of the Sigurd story are recorded on crosses from Maughold, Andreas and Michael, and so it is clear that this legend must have been a special favourite among the Norse settlers in Man.

Another famous example of the Scandinavian crosses is the handsome Thor Cross, from Bride, which Kermode describes as 'the richest example anywhere known of such illustrations of the old Norse mythology.' It is crowded with figures of all kinds—men, giants, birds, animals and dragons. On one side, Thor is shown attacking a serpent or dragon. There are also

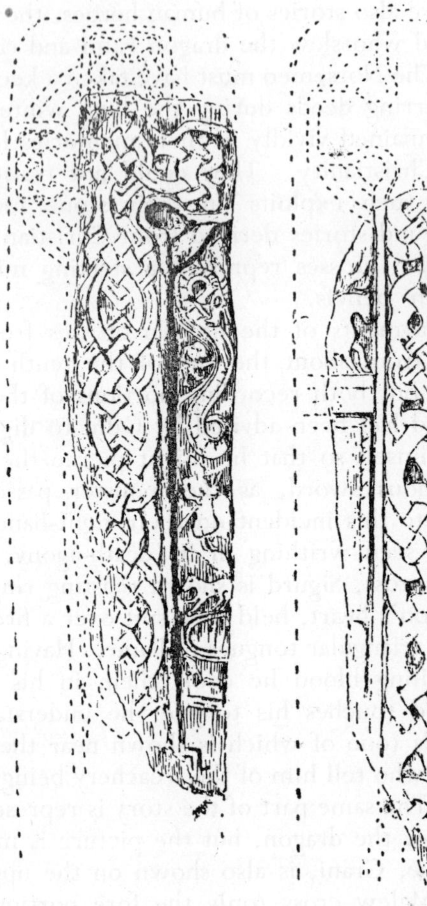

Fig. 29.—Fragments of Crosses from Jurby and Malew illustrating the Sigurd story

scenes from the mighty combat between Thor and the giant Rungnir. The god slew the giant but fell underneath him; and after all the other gods had failed to lift Thor up, his own son Main, though only three nights old, had the strength to do so, whereupon he received the giant's horse as a gift. On the other side is a scene from Thor's fishing adventure with the giant Hymi. Thor had been staying with the giant over-night, and when in the morning Hymi wished to go fishing, he would not help Thor to get any bait so that he could accompany him. The god, therefore, went to the giant's oxen and wrung the head off the largest of them. The picture on the right hand side of the cross, below the circle, shows Thor as a bearded man hurrying along and carrying the oxhead to be used as bait!

Thorwald's Cross, Andreas, symbolises the passing of these heathen beliefs and the coming of the Christian ideas. One side tells how ' Swart shall cast fire over the earth and burn the whole world . . . and the Powers shall perish.' The other side shows a Saint holding the Cross in one hand and the Holy Book in the other. He is treading on the serpent, and thus overcoming the powers of evil. The cross also has a figure of a fish, which was one of the earliest symbols of Christianity.

Of the 140 and more stone crosses so far discovered in Man only about forty-eight belong to the Scandinavian period. Most of them have been found in the northern parishes, including nine from Michael, and seven from each of Jurby and Andreas, while only two have been found in the sheading of Rushen. The distribution of the Celtic crosses is quite different, and the parish in which the greatest number has been found is Maughold, which has produced about thirty crosses of the earlier period but only seven of Scandinavian age.

The art of carving these stone crosses reached its height during the reign of Olaf I, but with the establishment and growth of Rushen Abbey, and the increasing influence of Rome, this type of monument came into disfavour. Latin was the language of the Church, and the Norse runes, as well as the whole art accompanying them, came to be regarded as something pagan. Hence in the early thirteenth century, that great art which had been practised in the Island for at least six centuries died away.

REFERENCES

(in addition to those given under Chapter IV).

KERMODE, P. M. C., *Manx Crosses*, London, 1907.

MARSTRANDER, C. J. S., *The Norwegian Conquest of the Isle of Man*, Oslo, 1932.

CUBBON, W. and MEGAW, B. R. S., The Western Isles and the Growth of the Manx Parliament, *Journal of the Manx Museum*, v (1942), 57-62.

FARRANT, R. D., *Mann, Its Land Tenure, Constitution and Deemsters,* London, 1937.

MEGAW, B. R. S., The Douglas Treasure Trove, *Journal of Manx Museum*, iv (1938), 77-82; also, Weapons of the Viking Age found in Man, *ibid.* III (1937), 234-7.

KERMODE, P. M. C., Ship-burial in the Isle of Man, *Antiquaries Journal*, x (1930), 126-133; also Knoc y Doonee, *Proc. I.M. Nat. Hist. and Antiq. Soc.*, III, (1928), 241-246.

CUBBON, W. C., History of Rushen Abbey, *Proc. I.M. Nat. Hist. and Antiq. Soc.*, IV, (1936), 98-115.

ELLIS, HILDA R., The Story of Sigurd in Viking Art, *Journal of the Manx Museum*, v (1942), 87-90; also, Sigurd in the Art of the Viking Age, *Antiquity*, xvi (1942), 216-274.

SHETELIG, H., Manx Crosses relating to Great Britain and Norway, *Saga Book of the Viking Society*, LX, (1925), 253-274.

KERMODE, REV. R. D., The Vikings in Man, *Journal of Manx Museum*, III (1925), 23-25 and 45-49.

Fig. 30.—Figure of the Norse God Heimdal blowing the Gjallar-horn.

(From one of the Jurby Crosses)

CHAPTER VI.

FROM THE NORSE KINGS TO THE STANLEYS (1266-1405)

WITH the year 1266 a profound change took place in the character of Manx history. It will be recalled that in that year, after the death of Magnus, the Island was definitely handed over to Alexander III of Scotland. This marked the beginning of a troubled era in the history of Man, since it was to fall a victim to the long struggle for supremacy between England and Scotland. So significant was the strategic position of the Island that both sides were anxious to gain possession of it. Hence it was tossed about like a shuttlecock between Scotland and England with neither side caring anything about its unfortunate inhabitants.

STRUGGLES BETWEEN SCOTS, MANX, AND ENGLISH

The Manx clearly showed their unwillingness to accept Scottish rule by rebelling under the leadership of Godred, son of King Magnus. A force led by John de Vesci arrived from Scotland to quell the revolt, and the Manx were outnumbered and heavily defeated in the battle on St. Michael's Island close to the landing place at Ronaldsway. Probably Godred himself fell in the battle, and if so, the encounter marked the end of the male descendants of the famous Godred Crovan, or King Orry.

Still more troubles were to come! Scotland was plunged into confusion in 1290 on the death of her very young queen, Margaret—called the Maid of Norway—who had succeeded her grandfather, Alexander III. There was a host of claimants for the Scottish crown, and there were also at least two ladies who claimed the Manx crown as being descendants of the former Kings of Man. The strong man of the period was then King Edward I of England, and he regarded the Island, which was said to be ' desolate and defenceless,' as an English possession, so that he took control of it. Meanwhile he had been invited to decide between the various claimants to the Scottish throne and, as is well known, he gave the crown to Balliol.

Being now King of Scotland, Balliol also took possession of the Isle of Man; but Edward I made it clear that the Scottish ruler was to pay homage to him for both Scotland and Man. Since Balliol refused to do this, warfare between England and Scotland followed in which Edward was victorious, Balliol was dethroned, and the Island once more came into English hands. The person appointed to govern Man was Antony Beck, the ambitious and warlike Bishop of Durham who had helped Edward in his battles against the Scots. Having once gained control over the Island, Beck quarrelled with Edward, but the latter died before anything was settled. Since the Bishop was a favourite of the weak Edward II, who succeeded his father, he was allowed to retain Man until his death in 1310,

In 1311 Piers Gaveston, a famous and evil figure in English history, was granted the Island by Edward II. But the wicked favourites of weak kings often have a very brief spell of power. The nobles drove Gaveston from his position and had him beheaded.

Bruce Visits Man (1313)

The unhappy Island was now to be the scene of still more strife and bloodshed. Bruce had become King of Scotland in 1313, and in the same year he came in person to take possession of Man. The Scottish force landed at Ramsey and proceeded via Douglas, where Bruce stayed at the Nunnery, on to Castle Rushen, which had become the great stronghold of the Island. After a month's siege the garrison surrendered, and the Castle was largely destroyed. Bruce granted Man to Thomas Randolph, Earl of Moray.

Irish Raiders

Before returning to Scotland, Bruce had made an expedition against Ireland; and in 1316, perhaps by way of revenge, a body of Irish freebooters under Richard de Mandeville appeared at Ronaldsway to pillage the land. The invaders scattered a Manx force on the slopes of South Barrule (then called Wardfell), and proceeded to ravage the surrounding countryside. Rushen Abbey must have formed an excellent prize for these raiders, and, according to the Manx *Chronicle*, it lost not only its furniture, but also its flocks and herds. When the Irish ultimately returned home, after a month's raiding, they were able to do so with their ships laden with choice plunder.

What a wretched period it all was for the Island! Who actually ruled the country between 1313 and 1333 it is well-nigh impossible to say; Scots and English appeared in succession, neither staying long. But after 1346 conditions became more stable, since the English, now under Edward III, dealt the Scots a decisive blow at the battle of Neville's Cross, and they were the effective masters of Man from that time onwards.

The Island Definitely Under England

In 1334 Edward III had granted the Island to William de Montacute, first Earl of Salisbury, in full possession, so that he became King of Man without having to pay homage to the English monarch. Montacute's son in 1392 sold the Island, including the crown, to William le Scrope, Earl of Wiltshire, who was beheaded by Henry IV. Man was next granted to the Earl of Northumberland, who was in turn deprived of it on being accused of treason; and finally, in 1405 it went to Sir John Stanley on condition of his doing homage, and giving two falcons at the coronation of each King of England. Stanley's descendants were destined to be rulers of Man, under the title of ' king ' or ' lord ' for over three hundred years.

The Church Grows in Power (1266-1405)

The condition of the people must have been utterly wretched during the unhappy period which has just been discussed, and there is little wonder that the Island was described as being poor and full of misery. Even the best rulers could do little since they stayed so short a time; and most who got possession of it merely regarded Man as a place from which they might take all they could to forward their own purposes.

While the civil power was weak and uncertain, the Church was constantly gathering strength. The Abbey of Rushen, and the bishopric, had received many grants of land and many valuable privileges from the Norse kings. Rushen was under the control of the Abbot of Furness. There was the Nunnery at Douglas with its Prioress; while lands in the Island were held by the Abbey of Bangor and Sabhal in northern Ireland, by the Priory of St. Bees in Cumberland, and the Priory of Whithorn in southern Scotland. The heads of these religious houses ranked as barons, and had their own officers and manorial courts.

As the power of the religious houses grew, so did that of the Pope as the head of the Christian Church, and the popes of those days were constantly striving for more and more power. Even in England papal interference was increasing. Powerful monarchs like Edward III found it difficult to resist papal claims, although many acts were passed to check them; but the Isle of Man had no strong ruler who could assist in curbing the power of the church.

The Abbot of Rushen alone held 99 quarterlands or farms, 66 mills and 77 cottages; and in connection with these holdings he had his own courts, over which his steward presided. The bishop wielded a power almost equal to that of a king. He had his own courts and judges (called vicars-general), and his own prison on Peel Island. Moreover, the church passed its own laws, and had an advantage over the state because its laws were put into writing. There were no written laws of the Island itself before 1422, but the written laws of the Manx church go back to 1229 when Bishop Simon held a diocesan synod at Kirk Braddan. At this synod, tithes for the clergy had been levied on livestock, grain, beer, and woven cloths. In 1291 another synod was held under Bishop Mark, and fresh tithes were also imposed on merchants and craftsmen.

In 1299 Mark was expelled from Man by Edward I, and the Pope replied by placing the Island under an interdict for three years. This was a punishment very much dreaded in those days since it meant that all church services ceased. When Bishop Mark returned to the Island in 1302, to show his authority, as well as to exact further punishment, he imposed a tax of one penny a year on every house with a fireplace. This tax lasted for centuries and was known as ' the smoke penny.'

Tithes

The tithes which had to be paid to the church covered all produce—grain, beer, animals, geese, poultry, eggs, butter, cheese, and fish—and the collection of these dues was carried out by the parson or his agent, called the proctor, while there were officers called sumners for enforcing payment. In the case of grain, which was the most important crop, the farmer must

Fig. 31.—Castletown—aerial view

Fig. 32.—Peel Castle—aerial view

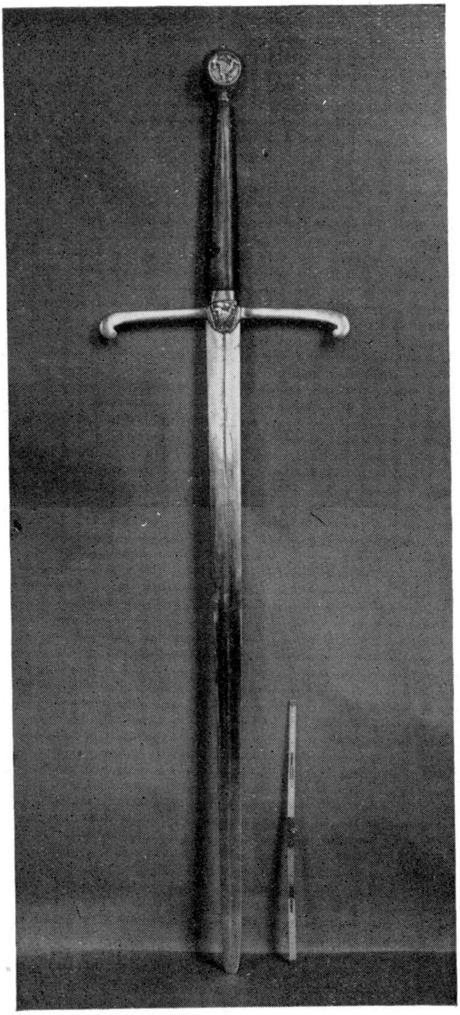

Fig. 33.—Manx Sword of State probably dating to the middle of the thirteenth century, or a little earlier, and bearing crest of Three Legs on the pommel and at the top of the blade. Now kept in Manx Museum.

Fig. 34.—The Pommel of Manx Sword of State, showing the Three Legs

Fig. 35.—Castle Rushen, from a print by Chaloner, about 1650.

The original description reads:—The prospective of Castel Rushen on the south east side. *A*. The inner ward of the Castle. *B*. The wall of the Castle. *C*. The wall aboute the Castle. *D*. The counterscarpe. *E*. The new building wherein the Earle of Derby lived. *F*. The new worke. *G*. The Burne that the sea comes in. *H*. As the towne appears.

not stack his corn without notice to the proctor. If he did so, then the sumner and two neighbours were to take the stack down and seize the tithe. Certain tithes such as butter, cheese and eggs had to be brought to the church on Sunday and handed to the parson at the altar; and the time came when the priest would stop people from receiving the sacrament because they had not paid these duties.

Of all the tithes paid in Man nearly half went to the bishop, who thus had the chief power. Of the remaining portion about half went to the religious houses, chiefly Rushen Abbey, and the rest was divided amongst the parish clergy.

Offenders against the church could be sent to the bishop's prison. For more serious offences against church discipline the punishment was excommunication, which meant that the guilty person was excluded from the church and its privileges. Like the interdict this was regarded as a dreadful penalty, but, in addition, the offender had to pay a money fine which went to the bishop.

As proof of the increasing power of the Pope throughout this period, it is significant that the bishop of Sodor and Man had now to go to Rome for consecration—a thing which the kings of England would not allow in the case of English bishops. Formerly the Manx bishops had been consecrated by the archbishop of Trondhjem, in Norway, but with Bishop Russell, who was elected in 1348, this practice ceased, and he was actually consecrated at Avignon, where the Pope resided at the time.

The Grey Friars

During Bishop Russell's term of office the Franciscan Friars came to the Island, for in 1373 they acquired a site in the parish of Arbory where they built an oratory. The Franciscans were sometimes called the Grey Friars because of their clothing, or Begging Friars, since they were not allowed to own property. They were rivals of the Cistercian Order to which the monks of Rushen Abbey belonged, and it may be supposed that they were encouraged in order to counteract the influence of the Abbey. Little is known of the doings of the Franciscans, but the remains of one of their buildings may be still seen at the Friary farm, in Ballabeg, Arbory.

Bishop Russell was succeeded in 1374 by Bishop Donkan, who was consecrated in Rome. For reasons that are rather obscure he got into trouble with the pope. It is probable that he made a stand in resisting papal greed and aggression, and in this he was playing the part of a patriot. He was transferred to another bishopric, possibly in Ireland, in 1392. Soon after this date, as already seen, a new era was to begin in Man, when, with the accession of the Stanleys, the power of the state was to increase, and that of the church to decline.

The Three Legs of Man

This was the period which saw the establishment of the Three Legs as the official crest of the Island. Many of the Norse kings, including Godred Crovan, Olaf I, and Harold I, had adopted the Viking ship as their emblem, but it is possible that towards the end of the Scandinavian period the crest of the Three Legs was also coming into use. At any rate it is certain that the device of the Legs was then known in the Island since it appears for the first time on the Manx Sword of State, which is still used at Tynwald ceremonies, and which dates back probably to the middle of the thirteenth century (Figs. 33 and 34). When Man came into Scottish hands, after 1266, King Alexander definitely adopted the design for his new possession, and its use has continued ever since.

The three legs is one of the most ancient of symbols, for it is seen on a Greek vase of the sixth century B.C. Like the more widespread swastika it is derived from a design showing the spokes of a wheel, which in turn represents the rays of the sun; and thus originally it was associated with sun worship. The design was taken to Sicily where it was adopted owing to the supposed appropriateness of the three legs to the shape of the island. The Scandinavians became familiar with Sicily, so it would not be surprising if they copied its badge and applied it to the Isle of Man. Further, the Scottish king, Alexander III, was intimately connected with Sicily, for his brother-in-law, Edmund, had the title of king of that island; and he took over the Sicilian design for the Isle of Man. The crest was, however, modified by the addition of spurs, while the legs were encased in armour, and it is in this altered form that the design of the Three Legs is now used. The Latin motto, *Quocunque Jeceris*

Stabit i.e. ' Whichever way you throw, it will stand ' was added later, being first seen on the earliest known Manx coinage, dating to 1668. (Compare Fig. 37).

Castle Rushen

The fortress of Castle Rushen existed in Norse times, since it is recorded that the last Norse king, Magnus, died there in 1265. It is therefore in origin a real Norse Castle although many of its features belong to the fourteenth century.

It has been pointed out that the Southside portion of Man contains a rich lowland area; and the mouth of the Silverburn river was a natural centre, and an obvious site for a fortification around which a town would grow. Castletown harbour was, nevertheless, always difficult for shipping, partly because the entrance is obstructed with limestone rocks, and partly because it is very exposed to south and south-west winds. The great harbour during Norse times was Ronaldsway, which was sheltered from the prevailing winds, and would provide good beaching for the war-galleys. On the other hand Ronaldsway had not a satisfactory supply of drinking water for the garrison of a castle, and vessels which landed there could be taken round when the weather became fine—or they might be dragged across the narrow peninsula—and could then lie safely under the protection of the castle walls. The earthwork at Hango Hill was very likely a halfway fort defending the road between Ronaldsway and Castletown.

Defensive works of some kind, perhaps an earth-mound surrounded by wooden palisades, have certainly existed at Castletown for many centuries. In Magnus' time the castle was built of stone, and was a square tower or keep in the late Norman style, probably constructed during the reign of Godred II (1153-1187). This tower was captured by Bruce, but portions can be seen in the present keep. The first additions were the lower parts of the south and west towers, which were probably made during the reign of Reginald I (1187-1226). Next followed some sections which are regarded as being in the finest style of the Castle, including the heightening of the original keep and its two added towers (south and west), an entirely new tower to the east side of the keep, and a twin-towered gate-tower built on the north side of the keep. These date to between about 1340 and 1350 during the reigns of the first and second Earls of Salisbury. Some of the architectural features in the sandstone doorways and windows closely resemble those used in later parts of the Edwardian castles of North Wales, particularly Beaumaris and Caernarvon, and there is reason for believing that Welsh craftsmen were brought over to help in strengthening Castle Rushen. In 1377 the French attacked it but failed to take it since the castle was now well able to withstand a siege. To the later years of the reign of the second Earl of Salisbury (1344-1392) belong the curtain wall with its parapet walk as well as the uppermost third or quarter of the keep—the latter having had to be raised in order to enable the defenders to fire over the wall-walk of the curtain.

During the Stanley regime, the castle with its garrison was the main centre of the Island's administration, and one of the most famous of the Stanleys, James, the seventh Earl of Derby, lived in it for several years (Fig. 35).

The actual Derby House was originally constructed during the later sixteenth century, but it was heightened and perhaps almost rebuilt in 1644 at the time of the Great Earl. In the eighteenth and nineteenth centuries, when the keep came to be used as a prison, the building was very much altered although at the same time it was preserved from falling into ruin. Nowadays it is used for holding the fortnightly courts, while new governors also continue to be installed there; otherwise the castle is essentially a show place.

Peel Castle

This was the Island's other fortress and administrative centre; and the islet on which it is erected, standing at the entrance to a good natural harbour, made it an admirable defensive site.* It lacked the richer economic basis available to the southern capital, and, facing west, it is more exposed to bad weather.

This islet, so famous under the name of St. Patrick's Isle, is the centre of much of the Island's early religious and civil history, and it well merits the description of 'The Tara of the Isle of Man' bestowed upon it by a thirteenth century Irish writer. Unlike Castle Rushen, its history, which has by no

*It is to this location that it owes its alternative name *Holme*—a Norse word for 'an islet in a bay, creek, lake or river' (J. J. Kneen).

means yet been entirely unravelled, is complicated by the existence of both ecclesiastical as well as military buildings, and only the more significant features can be mentioned here.

Of the existing masonry the earliest is the Round Tower, dating to the tenth or the early eleventh century, and occupying a prominent position on the islet. Built of well-jointed and squared blocks of local red sandstone it forms a splendid example of the refuge towers erected by the Celtic clergy to protect themselves and the treasures of their churches from the ravages of the Vikings. The tower has all the characteristic features of the Irish structures apart from the conical stone roof; and no doubt the original one collapsed to be replaced in mediaeval times by a battlemented top. The ancient parish church of St. Patrick and the Cathedral Church of St. German, both now in ruins, have already been noted (see p. 71, and Fig. 32).

On the military side the details of the earlier history of the island are still obscure, and further excavation is necessary before anything definite is said. But in any case it is clear that the actual name *Peel*, which early provided an alternative name for St. Patrick's Isle, and also gave its name to the settlement which ultimately grew up on the other side of the harbour mouth, originally meant 'a moated and palisaded enclosure, or a fort built of massive baulks of timber.' The earliest timber fort to which the title was applied was presumably the one erected by King Magnus Barefoot on the occasion of his visit to Man between 1098 and 1103 (see p. 53), and which was still, according to the Manx *Chronicle*, known by his name in 1260. Just what part of the islet was occupied by the fort is a matter for speculation. It has been suggested that the earthwork in the middle of St. Patrick's Isle was the site—but this was proved by excavation in 1947 to belong to the Derby period. On the other hand it may be observed that for the greater part of its length, there is a bank of earth on the inner side of the great ring line of fortification around the islet, and this no doubt formed part of the defences of earth and timber in the eleventh or twelfth century.

Of the masonry in the existing curtain wall enclosing the islet, the earliest dates to about 1300 A.D. and is situated to the south-east of the chancel of the Cathedral. Further work in this section as well as the rectangular tower overlooking the causeway linking the islet to the mainland are probably to be ascribed to Sir William le Scrope (Earl of Wiltshire) soon after 1392. The rest of the massive fortifications encircling the island, consisting of very large blocks of quarried slate, were probably erected by Thomas, first Earl of Derby, in the period between 1460 and 1504. Such defences may have been partly justified by the fear of Scottish raids, but they may also, as suggested by O'Neil, the Chief Inspector of Ancient Monuments, be regarded as another example of that ' grandiose expression of feudal pride ' which is rather characteristic of the period in question.* Unlike Castle Rushen, Peel Castle has become a ruin since the disbanding of its garrison in the eighteenth century.

REFERENCES

MOORE, A. W., *History*, I, pp. 181-208.

CLUCAS, G. F., Sir William le Scrope, *Mannin*, v, 1915, pp. 257-262, (with portrait).

CRADOCK, Rev. H. C., The Pre-Reformation Bishops of Sodor, *Proc. I.M. Nat. Hist. and Antiq. Soc.*, III, 1931, pp. 321-346.

RIGBY, A., *Castle Rushen*, Douglas, 1927.

DOUGLAS, J. E., *Castle Rushen*, Douglas, 1925.

CLUCAS, G. F., *Peel Castle*, Douglas, 1928.

*I wish to thank Mr. B. H. St. J. O'Neil for permission to use his archaeological reports on Castle Rushen and Peel Castle, which, unfortunately, have not yet been published.

Chapter VII.

THE FIRST STANLEYS
(1405-1627)

The gift of the Island to Sir John Stanley by King Henry IV marked the beginning of a new and better era in Manx history, for peace and stable government replaced the wars and anarchy of the preceding period. The Stanleys, who became the Earls of Derby after 1485, were a powerful and highly placed English family; and though they rarely visited the Island themselves, they appointed responsible governors who, in the main, seem to have aimed at carrying out their tasks with justice. Until 1504 the new rulers retained the title of king of Man, but this was then changed to lord of Man.

The Work of Sir John Stanley II
(1414-1432)

The first ruler of the Stanley line never came to Man, but the second Stanley took a great interest in his kingdom and visited it with very beneficial results for the Island. With him, indeed, began the first systematic record in writing of the history of Man, for it was he who introduced written laws, while he also curbed the power of the church, and restored the ancient constitution of the country. It has been shown that the most striking feature of the preceding period had been the immense growth in the power of the church and the weakening of the civil power. The church was dominated by the great barons, of whom the chief were the bishop, and the abbot of Rushen, and it was obvious to Sir John Stanley that he could never be the real ruler of the Island until the barons' power was checked. A beginning was made by forbidding them to give shelter—sanctuary it was called—to wrongdoers who tried to escape from justice by fleeing on to land held by the church, and thus claiming its protection. Next, the bishop and other barons were ordered to attend at a Tynwald held at Reneurling (now Cronk Urley) to give obedience to the new king. When three of them, namely, the prior of Whithorn, the abbot of Furness, and the prior of St. Bees, failed to do so, they were punished by being deprived of their lands in the Island.

Sir John Stanley then proceeded to codify the laws, and in this code, which was drawn up by the Deemsters and Keys, the relative rights and duties of the king, church and the people were defined for the first time. Of the Keys it was stated that their existence had been uncertain since the Scandinavian period (or, as it was expressed, 'since King Orry's days') during which they had consisted of twenty-four freeholders. It was also laid down that the king, or lord, had the right to veto the appointment of any member of the body. By the same code, the Council and Deemsters were to aid the Governor in all cases of difficulty, and the clerk of the rolls, in order to settle the law, was ordered to write all proceedings plainly so that a record of cases could be kept. Hitherto, as previously explained, the law had depended on the memory of the Deemsters and the Keys. Trial by combat, or prowess, was abolished, and trial by jury (or, as it was then called, by God and the country) was adopted in its place. Although the second Sir John Stanley was a despotic ruler he was also a wise and bold one, and what he did left an enduring mark on the Island.

Absentee Rulers

For almost a hundred years after the death of the second Stanley, Man saw nothing of its rulers. The second Earl of Derby (1504-1521), who was the first to give up the title of king and become lord of Man, visited the Island in 1507 to put an end to some 'public tumult' that had taken place. Nothing is known of the origin or nature of this 'tumult,' but it is mentioned in an old Manx ballad. The Earl, who had been raiding the Scottish coast of Kirkcudbright, possibly in revenge for a previous attack by the Scots on Man, landed at Ronaldsway and soon quelled the rising. It was on the occasion of this visit that the port of Derbyhaven received the name it still holds.

The third Earl (1521-1572) never came to the Island, but during the course of his long reign, certain grievances of the people against demands of the church were settled. This was in 1532 when it was agreed that the tithe on ale and on all marriage presents, which had been paid to the church, should be abolished, while the death dues were reduced.

The Peaceful Reformation

During the period of the third Earl of Derby's lordship in Man, the important religious changes known as the Reformation were taking place in England. The great break with Rome occurred, and Henry VIII became the supreme head of the Church of England in 1534, while shortly afterwards the monasteries were suppressed. The Act of 1539, by which the lands of the English religious houses were confiscated, did not mention the Island, and consequently did not extend to it, nor was any statute dealing with the matter passed in Man. Nevertheless, the Manx monasteries were suppressed soon after those in England, and all the property belonging to Rushen Abbey, the Nunnery of Douglas, and the Friary of Bemaken (Ballabeg, Arbory), was seized by the Crown, while the buildings gradually fell into ruin.

It took some time for the new religious ideas to be accepted in the Island, since, in 1594, orders were issued to the vicars-general to bring to trial all persons carrying bells or banners before the dead, or praying for the dead. It was not until 1610 that the Manx clergy were free to marry, whereas the English clergy had been allowed to do so since 1549. This slowness of the Manx Reformation was partly due no doubt to the fact that its ruler, the third Earl, was a strong Roman Catholic; but the main reasons were probably the relative isolation of Man, together with the ignorance of the English language, and the lack of any books in the Manx tongue.

The Island under Queen Elizabeth and James I (1594-1610)

After the death of the fifth Earl of Derby, in 1594, a dispute arose as to who should be the new lord of Man. While the dispute was proceeding Queen Elizabeth took control of the Island, and she and her successor, James I, continued to appoint its governors until 1610. It is said that during her period of control, Queen Elizabeth presented to Castle Rushen the ancient clock which still adorns its walls, and does duty as the town clock of Castletown.

In 1612 the rule of the Derbys was restored when the sixth Earl and his Countess, Elizabeth, began to rule jointly. The government of the Island was entirely in the hands of the Countess, but neither of them visited Man. On the death of the Countess, in 1627, the control of the Island was taken over by their son Lord Strange, who was to become the seventh Earl of Derby in 1642. His period of rule is the most memorable in the whole of the Stanley regime, as will be seen in the next chapter, and he came to be known as 'The Great Stanley.'

Social and Economic Conditions (1405-1627)

What sort of life was lived by the farmers and fishermen, the farm labourers and artisans during these two centuries? Almost the only information we have is contained in the book of the Statutes, and it suggests that the Island's rulers were more anxious for the lord's privileges and his revenues than for the people's welfare. Many of these 'statutes' are mere records of old customs in the state and the church, while others are decrees made by the lord or his officers. The Keys at that time were not really the makers of laws; their duties were those of a supreme jury rather than those of a parliament. They were not called together regularly, nor even frequently. Thus, no laws were passed between 1430 and 1504; and the whole record of the laws, customs and ordinances, up to the end of the sixteenth century covers only some seventy pages in the statute book.

The Lord's Privileges

The lord had the right to receive the 'royal' fish of porpoise, sturgeon, and whale, to take the better sort of game such as hawk, heron, hart or hind, all wrecks and treasure trove, and the goods of persons condemned to death. He was also entitled to a very large quantity of free food for his castles (Rushen and Peel), each quarterland having to supply one beef per annum, which amounted to six hundred beeves a year, while there were 'customs' of corn and herring. Turf and ling had to be brought to the castles free. Not only did the lord claim toll on the produce of his subjects, but he also claimed to control their personal freedom. Thus no tenant could leave the Island without special licence, and if he did so he was to be treated as a felon and his goods forfeited. The reason for this was, no doubt, that tenants were not easy to find. Tenants had to labour on certain fixed days in repairing the lord's forts and houses. Taxes had to be paid for the liberty of fishing for herrings, for importing and exporting goods, and for grinding at the lord's mills. To avoid going to the latter, many people used hand-mills, or querns, which were seized and destroyed by the lord's order whenever they could be found.

Watch and Ward

There was universal military service in those days, and all men between twenty and sixty years had to train as militiamen under the captains of the parishes. The weapons used were bows and arrows, the sword and buckler, and every man had to provide himself with them. Moreover, practically every man was obliged to take his turn in keeping 'watch and ward' at the various watch-stations, both by day and night, for an enemy that might approach (Fig. 36). Great stress was laid on this duty, and very severe penalties were imposed for any neglect in carrying it out. The only men exempted from watch and ward were some of the chief officials together with 'one head smith, the head or chief miller in every parish,' and even they had 'to be ready to encounter the enemy.' It was, however, laid down that only those should be sent on watch who were 'of discretion and able to discern and to be careful.' The means of summoning in turn the men required for this service has never been described in detail, but it is known from various records that there were recognised watch tokens, in the form of a cross, which passed from house to house within the parish, and were accepted as a stern summons.

Strict rules were laid down for the hiring of farm labourers and servantmaids. The usual form of hiring was by the year, men servants being hired in November and women in May. Deemsters and other officers had the right of forcibly hiring or 'yarding' one male and one female servant 'or more if it be needful for them' from each sheading. As some return for this enforced service, such servants were entitled to have their porridge made so thick that the pot-stick would stand upright in the middle of the pot. Tenants who had difficulty in obtaining servants could appeal for the help of the deemster through the coroner; and if no 'vagrant' servants were

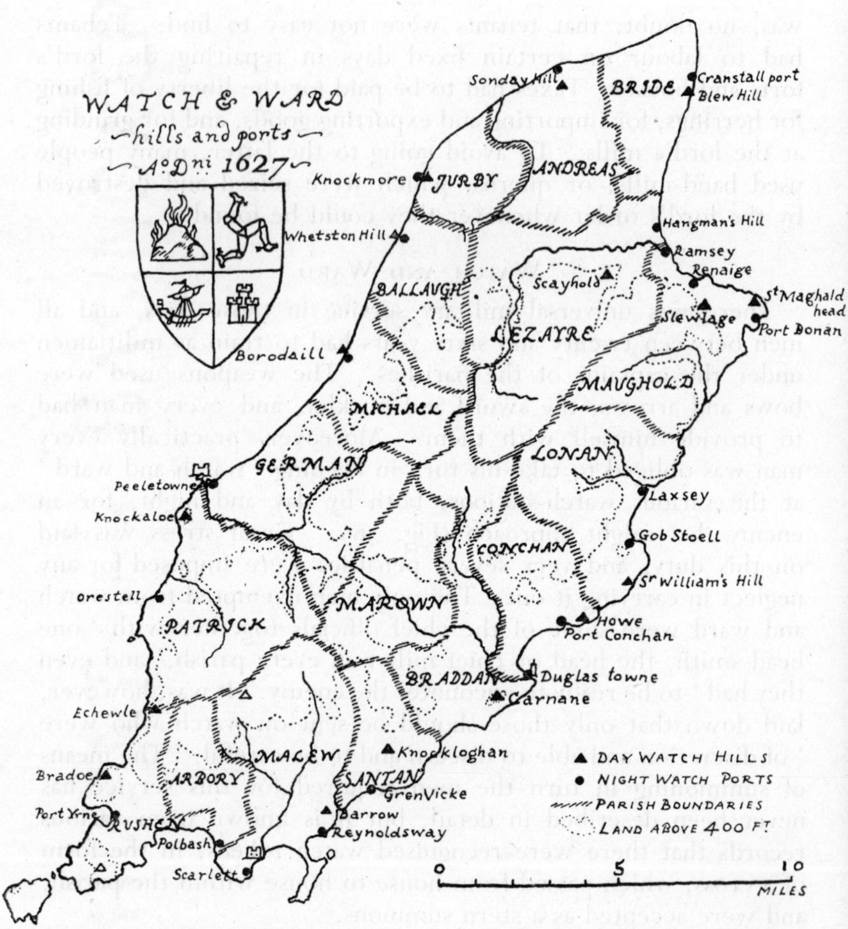

Fig. 36.—Map showing positions of day and night-watch stations recorded in an official document of 1627. The coat of arms, which shows a beacon-hill ablaze, the Legs of Man and the galley of the Lord of the Isles, was borne by the family MacLeod of Cadboll (Cromarty), who claimed to be descended from the Kings of Man and the Isles

available, then the tenants paying a lower rent had to serve those paying a higher rent, 'rather than that the lord's land should fall into decay.'

Parents who were old, disabled, or sick were allowed to retain one of their children, called a 'choice-child,' at home, but only if they gave public notice at the parish church, at least a month before hiring day. Servants who refused to carry out their duties were liable to whipping and being sent to gaol. Though whipping has long been out of use, imprisonment of farm-labourers who broke their contracts was common until quite recently; but while the law permitting imprisonment is still unrepealed, it has become a dead letter.

REFERENCES

GILL, J. F., (Editor), *Statutes of the Isle of Man,* London, 1883.
MOORE, A. W., *History of the Isle of Man*, I, 211-230.
CUBBON, W., Watch and Ward, in 1627, *Proc. I.M. Nat. Hist. and Antiq. Soc.*, III, 1928, pp. 258-265.
MEGAW, B. R. S., A Thousand Years of Watch and Ward, *Journal of the Manx Museum*, V (1941), pp. 8-13.
WALPOLE, SPENCER, *The Land of Home Rule*, London, 1893.

Fig. 37.—The Three Legs taken from the Manx Coinage, 1733

Chapter VIII.

THE GREAT STANLEY AND ILLIAM DHONE

(1627-1663)

The period covered by this chapter was a very memorable one for the Isle of Man, no less than for England. Stirring events were taking place 'across the water,' since the vital struggle between King and Parliament was in progress, leading ultimately to the Civil War, the execution of Charles I (1649), and the establishment of the English Commonwealth, which lasted until 1660. Whatever its own wishes might have been, the Island was bound to be involved in the English struggle, since its ruler, the seventh Earl of Derby, was the head of a great royalist family who felt in honour bound to give active support to the King. On the other hand, the sympathies of a great many of the Manx must have been with the Parliament, since they had many grievances against their own rulers. This feeling of discontent found expression in the rebellion of William Christian (*Illiam Dhone*), which led to the execution of this Manx patriot in 1663.

The Great Stanley (Yn Stanlagh Mooar)

(1627-1651)

James, the seventh Earl of Derby, was a remarkable man, as may be judged for the title he earned for himself in the Island as the Great Stanley, or, *Yn Stanlagh Mooar* (Fig. 39). He was barely twenty-one when his father gave him the government of Man, and he began by doing something which had not been done by any of his predecessors—choosing a Manxman as his lieutenant-governor. The person chosen was Edward Christian of Maughold, a man of great ability who had lived a life of adventure. He had been a captain in the service of the East India Company, a courtier in the suite of the Duke of Buckingham, and a commander of a naval frigate. Finally, he retired to his native Isle with a considerable fortune, and had acquired the mine workings at Bradda Head.

This is how the Earl, in writing to his son years later, described him:—'I was newly got acquainted with Captain Christian, whom I soon observed to have abilities enough to do me service . . . but which took most with me, when he offered his service it was on these terms, that he would be content to hold the staff until I chose another. For the pay, he so little valued that, as he would be content to do service without any or as little of it as it pleased me. He is excellent company, as rude as a sea captain should be, but refined as one that hath civilised himself half a year at court.' But these professions of caring nothing about the pay were too good to be true. Christian was dismissed in 1639, and the reason given by the Earl was that 'the more I gave, the more he asked.'

Civil War in England and Unrest in Man

On the outbreak of the Civil War in England, Lord Strange, as his title then was, raised an army of 5,000 men to fight for Charles, and equipped them at his own expense. He also gave the King large sums of money, and rendered many important services in the field. In spite of all this he was distrusted by Charles, whose advisers seemed to look on him as a rival for the throne.

The troubles in England were, in a smaller way, being repeated in Man. Edward Christian had been partly restored to favour, and had been given command of the Manx forces. He formed a training camp at the Lhen, Jurby, and, if we may trust the evidence given against him afterwards at his trial, stirred up the soldiers to rebel against the Earl. But the trouble was not confined to the armed forces; the feeling of discontent about paying tithes had again become acute, and the governor, fearing an insurrection, invited each parish to send representatives to state their grievances. Instead of this the whole population was summoned by the sending round of the muster cross, or *Crosh Vusta*, and they came bearing arms, to the terror of the court. The governor tried to put them off by promising to give them a hearing another day, but they answered that they desired no other day, and a man named William Garett, of Sulby, declared that the country would pay no more tithes but would fight and die first. The governor appeased them by promising to send for Lord Derby.

When the Earl came he brought with him a small troop of English cavalry. This, in his own words, is how he dealt with the threatened revolt: 'When first I came among the people,

I seemed affable and kind to all, so I offended none. For taking off your hat, a good word, a smile or the like, will cost you nothing, but may gain you much.' The meeting of parish representatives was then held and the Earl was told of the people's grievances. He next summoned the officers, the twenty-four Keys, and four men from every parish to Peel Castle to aid him in settling the complaints. Edward Christian and the ringleaders of the disturbances were present at this meeting, which threatened to be a stormy one. Lord Derby was equal to the occasion. 'There were some,' he wrote, 'who saucily behaved themselves, and of those I put some out of countenance with austere looking on them; troubling their discourse in seeming not to hear well what they said and asking them to repeat the same; which astonished them so, that oft they did forget the matter they were about, and sometimes feared to speak more of it . . . Another sort were more dangerous, who said nothing openly but instructed others and whispered behind the company. Some of these I espied myself; others were pointed to me by such as I had set in several places about the bench, to observe them and give me some private beck, which I took notice of as I saw occasion. These I called nearer to the bar, who it may be, would speak so as not to offend, or hold their peace; at least there they could not incite others so conveniently.'

In the end, the meeting agreed to leave the settlement of their grievances to the Earl himself. Christian, who saw himself being outwitted, rose to call attention to some questions which had been overlooked, but Lord Derby promptly ruled him out of order and declared the meeting at an end. Shortly after this, Christian was arrested and cast into prison to await trial on a charge of treason. He was charged with attempting to overthrow the government, to make the House of Keys an elected body, to have the deemsters chosen every three years from among the Keys, and to impose a new oath on both Keys and deemsters to repeal all laws not in the interests of the people.

Christian had no doubt counted upon winning power by a sudden stroke, and then declaring openly for Cromwell and the Parliament. He had failed, and the penalty was a fine of a thousand marks, and imprisonment for life. He remained in gaol until 1651 when the Parliament forces entered the Island. In 1659 he

Fig. 38.—Peel Castle, from a print by Chaloner, about 1650

The original description reads:—Peel Castle as it doth appeare from the east. *A*. The hill yt is farr hier than the Castle. *B*. The sea that comes round about the Castle. When the tide is at highest the greatest shipps may runne about it and come into ye harbour, and when ye tide is out maie goe drie to the Castle. *C*. The Rocks. *D*. The Hill with-in the Castle. *E*. The Wall aboute the Castle. *F*. The Cathedrall Church. *G*. Two other chappells. The rest are lodgings. The hills are the landskipp of Wale (*sic*) and Ireland.

Fig. 39.—James Stanley, seventh Earl of Derby (1607-1651). 'The Great Earl'

Fig. 40.—Castle Mona

Fig. 41.—King William's College

Fig. 42.—Farm-house Kitchen in the Manx Museum, showing characteristic equipment

was concerned in a plot against Governor Chaloner and was again sent to prison in Peel Castle, where he died in 1661.

To some extent the Earl satisfied the people by securing a reduction of tithes and other payments to the clergy. But he created another, and even more serious grievance, which was destined to be a sore in the Island's life for the next sixty years. Though the lord had always claimed the full ownership of the soil, there was an ancient system by which the 'tenants' had been able to pass on the farms to their children, and to dispose of them to other people. Lord Derby now planned to establish a system of leases by which no family could claim to hold a piece of land for longer than three lives.

Lord Derby's Royalist Activities

The full effects of this policy were not yet realised, however, and the tithe trouble for the time settled, Lord Derby was free to give his full attention to increasing the military forces and strengthening the defences of the Island. He raised a troop of cavalry consisting in all of 288 men; the foot soldiers were constantly drilled, and the garrisons of Castle Rushen and Peel Castle were strengthened. Seven camps were formed, three in the North, and four in the South, of the Island. New forts were also erected, one at Fort Island, called Derby Fort, another at Ramsey, called Fort Loyal, and a third at the Point of Ayre. There was also a large earthwork at Ballachurry in the parish of Andreas.

At sea, Lord Derby raised and equipped a small fleet which from time to time came into conflict with opposing ships. On one occasion they defeated five men-of-war, and on another defended the Calf of Man from an attack by three Parliamentary ships. The burden of these increased armaments by land and by sea bore heavily on the people, who grew more and more discontented as time went on. This feeling was, no doubt, aggravated by the disasters which befel the Royalist cause.

After the execution of Charles I, in 1649, the Earl was offered the return of his English estates if he would surrender the Island to Parliament. He indignantly refused. 'If you trouble me with any more such messages,' said he, 'I will burn the paper and hang the bearer.' So, when in 1651 an attempt was made to regain the crown for Charles II, the Earl hastened to join the royal standard. The small Manx force of 300 foot soldiers which he took with him, was attacked near Wigan and overwhelmed by superior numbers. The Earl made good his escape, succeeded in joining the King's army, and shared in the rout of Worcester. He was taken prisoner, and although his life had been promised him by his captors, he was tried by court martial and executed at Bolton in 1651.

Whatever his faults, the Great Stanley was a man of 'loyal nature and of noble mind.' In spite of great discouragement, he adhered to the cause of his king, and was not afraid to die for it. Yet the Stuart period was not one in which we might expect to find the perfect ruler. The Earl was masterful and grasping. Like his royal master, he tried to quell opposition by force, and he was not above that kind of diplomacy which could more bluntly be called artfulness. His land laws left a legacy of hate, but in imposing them he was acting in the manner of other great English noblemen. What he has written about the Isle of Man shows that once the people had recognised his position as not only their lord, but their landlord, he was anxious to do what he could for their welfare. Though a most devout churchman, he tried to remedy the exactions of the church. His loyalty to the king, natural as it was, placed the Island under great burdens and in great danger for the sake of a cause which was not really its own.

The Rebellion of Illiam Dhone
(1651)

When Lord Derby had set sail on that fatal expedition in 1651, he had left the Island under the care of his Countess, Charlotte. She was a woman of great courage and constancy, as she had proved by her heroic defence of Lathom House for over two years against the forces of the Parliament. One of her principal officers was William Christian, who held the offices of receiver of the revenues and major-general. There were other officers in command of the castles, but Christian trained the unpaid native soldiers, the militia. This William Christian, or *Illiam Dhone* (brown-haired William), as his countrymen familiarly called him, was a son of Deemster Ewan Christian and a distant relative of Edward Christian, the former governor.

When the news came of the Earl's defeat and capture, the Manx seized the opportunity to try and get their grievances regarding the land leases and the free quartering of troops remedied. On October 19th, some eight hundred of them, including the leading men in the various parishes, met at Illiam Dhone's residence at Ronaldsway, and took an oath ' that the people should withstand the Lady of Derby until she had yielded to their aggreavances.' They were told that the Countess, without their knowledge, had sent to make conditions of peace, and that she ' would sell them for twopence apiece.' It was true that she had written to Colonel Duckenfield, the commander of the force which Parliament had now sent to capture the Island. Duckenfield's expedition set out from Chester the day before the Ronaldsway meeting, but, owing to bad weather, it did not reach Ramsey for a week. Christian and the militia had in the meantime obtained possession of all the forts, except Rushen and Peel, and had sent a message to Duckenfield offering to surrender Man on condition that the islanders ' might enjoy their lives and liberties as formerly they had.' He and his associates did not trust the Countess to think about the Island's constitution and customs!

Parliamentary Forces in Man

Duckenfield sent one section of his forces to take Peel, while he himself prepared to besiege Castle Rushen. He first summoned the Countess to surrender, and in the letter referred to ' the late Earl of Derby.' This was the first news Lady Derby had heard of her husband's death, and she was ' extremely affected.' She sent a message offering to surrender, but on terms more suited to a victor than to one in her hopeless situation. Duckenfield's reply was to bring up his cannon and make ready for the attack. Part of the garrison attempted flight by leaping from the battlements, while others made a breach in the walls and admitted the attackers to the outer ramparts. Seeing that the end had come, Lady Derby surrendered on the sole condition that the lives of the defenders should be spared, and that she and her family should have liberty to go to England to seek terms from the Parliament. The resistance might have been much prolonged if only the garrison had had any heart in the defence, because Castle Rushen was immensely strong, and was well provided with arms and munitions. This was well known to the besiegers, who were greatly relieved when the place fell so easily into their hands.

Illiam Dhone has sometimes been called a patriot, and sometimes a rebel and traitor. That he was disloyal to the Countess, and betrayed a great trust reposed in him, cannot be denied. But he considered that he owed a greater duty to his own Manx countrymen, and that if the Countess had been allowed to make resistance, the Island would have been conquered by bloodshed and its ancient liberties taken away. At the same time it seems clear that he, and those who joined in the Ronaldsway plot, intended in any case to change or to coerce their rulers. If they hoped to secure their old ownership of the land they were, however, to be disappointed, for under the Commonwealth government nothing of this nature was changed.

The Island under the English Parliament

In anticipation of final victory, Parliament had already granted Man to Lord Fairfax, under whom governors continued to administer the Island in accordance with its old constitution. The best known of these governors was James Chaloner, who wrote a short history of the Island which has been reprinted in the Manx Society's publications. He acted as head of the Manx Church, since the bishops were abolished in Man as well as in England, and used the bishop's salary partly in founding schools in the four towns. During Chaloner's governorship, William Christian was accused of being short in his accounts, and he retired to estates which he had in Lancashire. This was early in 1659, the year when Cromwell died. The army was in disagreement with Parliament, and the commander of Peel Castle seized Chaloner and imprisoned him. In this the commander had the assistance of Edward Christian, and also, it is alleged, of William Christian. Parliament recovered its power and ordered Chaloner's release. He was in office at the time of the Restoration, but died shortly afterwards.

The Restoration of The Derbys (1660)

The restoration of Charles II was announced in Peel, Castletown, Douglas and Ramsey with great rejoicings, and

Manxmen appear to have accepted the change back from the Commonwealth to the Monarchy as readily as they had adopted the previous change over. The rule of the Parliament had brought none of those benefits for which they had so fondly hoped. The land leases imposed by Earl James were still continued, and the condition of the people in general was, according to Chaloner, one of great poverty.

With the restoration of Charles Stuart came also the restoration of Charles Stanley, the eighth Earl of Derby, as Lord of Man. He restored the bishopric, and set about punishing the ringleaders in the rebellion against his mother, and above all, William Christian. Christian was then in London, a prisoner for a debt; but on his release he came back to the Island, believing that the general pardon granted by King Charles II extended to the Island. Despite this he was immediately arrested and brought to trial.

The Death of Illiam Dhone (1663)

Whether or not Christian was justified in his actions in 1651, there could be no doubt that he had broken the law, and, but for the king's pardon, had incurred the penalty of death. The argument of the Earl and his officers was that the pardon covered offences against the king of England, but not offences committed against the lord of Man. Christian denied the right of the court to try him and refused to plead, so that he was virtually condemned without trial. Several members of the House of Keys were unwilling to condemn him, and were removed, their places being filled by others. Before his trial Illiam Dhone had sent an appeal to the King in Council, but the appeal did not reach London until after he had been shot on Hango Hill. He made a fine end. He delivered an eloquent speech claiming that he had acted in the best interests both of the Countess and of the country. The soldiers offered to blindfold him so that he should not see the shots being fired, but he declined. It was said that most of the firing squad deliberately shot in the air, and that only one aimed true and killed him. He was mourned by the Manx as a martyr for his country, and a ballad *Baase Illiam Dhone* was written to commemorate him.

In the end the appeal to the king was upheld, William Christian's name was cleared, and his estates were restored to his family. Three other ringleaders of the rising, who had been imprisoned, were released, and their lands were returned to them.

REFERENCES

Illiam Dhone and the Manx Rebellion, Manx Society, xxvi, Douglas, 1877.

Stanley Legislation of Man, Manx Society, iii, Douglas, 1860.

CAINE, P. W., The Second Episode of Illiam Dhone, *Proc. I.M. Nat. Hist. and Ant. Soc.* iv (1938), 136-145.

MOORE, A. W., *History*, I, 231-280, 375-383; also *Manx Worthies*, Douglas, 1901.

MEGAW, B. R. S., The Fiery Cross and the Manx 'Crosh Vusta,' *Journal of the Manx Museum*, v (1941), 35-37.

Chapter IX.

THE LAST STANLEYS
(1660-1736)

THE LAND QUESTION AND THE FINAL STRUGGLE BETWEEN CHURCH AND STATE

Bishop Barrow

The restoration of the Derby rule in 1660 has already been described in the previous chapter, and it will be recalled that the first great event after the arrival of the eighth Earl was the trial of *Illiam Dhone*. Apart from this his period of rule was marked by the efforts of Bishop Isaac Barrow (1663-1671) to improve the position and education of the Manx clergy. The bishop was much shocked on his appointment to find that the clergy were, for the most part, ignorant and underpaid. The salaries of some of the vicars did not exceed £5 or £6 a year; and in order to make a living many were forced to engage in other occupations, including even the keeping of alehouses.

Their congregations understood only Manx, and as there were no books printed in this language, the clergy had to translate from the English Bible and Prayer Book as they went along, and many of them did not properly understand English. In order to help remedy this, he purchased the estate of Hango Hill and Ballagilley, in Malew, and gave it to trustees in order to found a school. This object was not fully accomplished until 1833, when King William's College was built on the site which the bishop had bought; and the principal endowment of that college is still called the Bishop Barrow Charity. In the meantime, young men intended for the church received scholarships at the ' academic ' school in Castletown.

Manx Coinage

On the death of Earl Charles the succession fell upon William, the ninth Earl (1672-1702). Until his time there had been no official coinage in the Island, and most of the coins in use were of Irish origin, being known by such names as ' St. Patrick's ' half-pence, or ' Limerick ' tokens. In 1668 John Murrey, a farmer and merchant who lived at Ronaldsway, had issued a copper coinage bearing his own name. These ' John Murrey ' pence were the first coins minted in the Island, and they were made legal by an Act of Tynwald in 1679.

The Land Question and the Act of Settlement (1704)

Throughout the ninth Earl's period of rule, the quarrel regarding the method of holding the land, which had been begun under the Great Earl, was continued with increasing bitterness. Farms were becoming empty, not only as a result of the uncertainty of the rights of landholders, but also because of a succession of bad harvests and poor fishing seasons which caused much emigration. Attempts to find new tenants met with scant success, and at last the Earl determined to deal with the matter in person. He crossed to the Island in 1699 and appointed Bishop Wilson, then in his second year of office, to receive proposals from the tenants for a settlement. Although nothing final could be accomplished before the Earl's death, it was the first business to be taken in hand by his brother and successor, James, tenth Earl, who was actually the last of the Stanleys. Bishop Wilson, in consultation with the Keys, had drawn up proposals to which the Earl's consent was obtained. These were embodied in the famous Act of Settlement of 1704, which is known as the Manx *Magna Carta*, by which the land question was finally settled.

The Manx System of Land-Holding

In order to appreciate the significance of this Manx Act it is necessary to look back a little to see what changes had taken place in the methods of holding land in the Island. It is believed that, at the beginning of the Stanley rule, the land was regarded as the property of the king, and that the land-holders, or tenants, simply held it from year to year without any right of inheritance.* As time passed on, it became customary for

*The nature of land tenure *before* the Stanley regime is a disputed and complicated one. The view adopted by Deemster Farrant in *Mann, Its Land Tenure*, etc. (1937), is that prior to the Scandinavian period, the tenure was Odal (or Udal), and that the land was held in hereditary right and not from the king. He further argues that this tenure remained essentially the same throughout the Scandinavian period, despite the legend of Godred Crovan who, according to the *Chronicle of Mann*, after the battle of Skyhill, divided the Island between his own followers and the surviving Manxmen on condition that ' none should ever presume to claim any of the land by hereditary right.' Thus the period when the Udal tenure fell into disregard was the dismal one between 1266 and 1405, when chaos prevailed for considerable intervals.

the lease to be renewed automatically until, in the end, the estates came to be regarded by the farmers as essentially their own possessions, from which they could not be turned out, but which they could sell if they wished, or hand on to their descendants. When land was sold, the seller gave the buyer a straw grown on the land, and the new owner was said to hold by the straw. This system of land tenure—known as the *straw tenure*—became well established, and was recognised in the Island courts. It should, however, be pointed out that the sale was carried out in the presence of the lord or his steward; and from the legal point of view, the straw was a symbol which really meant that one tenant was surrendering his holding to the lord, and that the latter was granting it to the incoming tenant or purchaser. Landholders had to pay the lord a fixed annual rent (known as lord's rent), and when the ownership changed, there was a kind of succession tax called an alienation fine.

This system of land holding was confirmed by James I of England in 1607, when he was in charge of Man; but when the seventh Earl of Derby came to live in the Island, like an English lord of the manor settled in the midst of his tenantry, he determined to put an end to all this. He ordered that all lands were to be held on lease, and that the leases lasted either for three lives or for twenty-one years. This meant that the rents could be altered from time to time, and thus a tenant could not be certain that his son would possess the land after him. Most of the inhabitants lived by farming, and so everyone felt insecure and discontented. This, more than anything else, was the real grievance which *Illiam Dhone* and his eight-hundred fellow-conspirators wished to redress when they deserted the Countess and threw in their lot with the Commonwealth.

By the Act of Settlement (1704), the so-called 'tenants' became in reality the owners of the land, possessing the rights of inheritance and of sale, and paying only the fixed lord's rent. The alienation fine was retained, but the irritating services which had grown up, such as supplying food and carrying turf to the castles, were abolished. In recent years, as the result of an Act passed in 1913, the lord's rent has been bought out by the payment of a lump sum. At the present time the British Crown, which now has the rights of the former lords, owns the minerals under the soil, and the slate and stone (subject to the landowner being allowed to take stone for the use of himself and his neighbour), and charges a royalty to those who work the mines and quarries. It also owns part of the mountain pastures which are let off for the rearing of large numbers of sheep.

Bishop Wilson (1698-1755)

Bishop Wilson, the most remarkable of all the rulers of the Church in Man, was 34 years of age on his appointment, and died in office fifty-seven years later at the advanced age of 91.

He was a man of saintly life; he took an active part in spreading Christianity in distant corners of the world; and he was selfless and fearless. His kindly acts brought him the love of the mass of the people. He devoted at least one-fifth of his income to pious uses, and when a great famine occurred, in 1739, and many people were in danger of dying from starvation, he not only gave away large quantities of grain from his own farms, but purchased cargoes for distribution to those in need. From the outset he refused to hold more than one church living at once because he could not personally attend to the duties involved. He did this at a time when pluralism, as it was called, was very common, and he did it although the income from the bishopric was only £400 a year. Late in life he was offered a richer see but nobly refused, saying, 'I will not leave my wife in her old age because she is poor.'

He rebuilt the bishop's palace (Bishopscourt), and took steps to repair the residences of the poorer clergy and to improve their stipends. He also had several churches rebuilt. He reformed the church in many ways, one of which was summoning the clergy to their convocation, or annual parliament, and preparing for their consideration a fresh code of ecclesiastical laws. Parents were compelled to send their children to school until they could read English distinctly, and thus the bishop was the pioneer of universal education in the British Isles. It was he, too, who began the printing of the Bible in the Manx language.

The Struggle Between Church and State

There was, unhappily, another side to Bishop Wilson's character which showed itself in his desire to revive the ancient power of the church and of the ecclesiastical courts. This battle between the church and the state began when the governor refused to allow the soldiers, who in those days performed the duties of policemen, to arrest persons sentenced by the vicars-general and take them to the bishop's prison in the damp crypt beneath St. German's Cathedral. It was carried further when the governor denied the right of the ecclesiastical courts to punish members of the castle households and garrisons, and when he allowed persons sentenced by the church to appeal to a civil court. The climax was reached in 1722, when the bishop passed a sentence upon the governor's wife, Mrs. Horne, who was held guilty of slander against another lady, and was ordered to make a public acknowledgement of her offence.

This was too much for Governor Horne. He had already drawn up a series of charges against the bishop and his vicars-general, and he now ordered them to cancel these and other recent proceedings as illegal. They refused, and were each heavily fined, and on failing to pay the fine were committed to prison in Castle Rushen. The bishop appealed to the King in Council, and after having been in prison for nine weeks, was released until the appeal could be heard. The decision did not arrive until two years later, and although partly in the bishop's favour, it did nothing to uphold the ecclesiastical rights for which he had fought. The governors who succeeded Horne were even more hostile to the claims of the church, and the bishop lived to see his cherished church discipline falling gradually into disuse.

The Rev. John Keble, in a biography of Bishop Wilson, has compared the bishop's conflict against the lord of Man with the conflict between Archbishop Thomas Becket and King Henry II of England, and it may be said that in many ways, as a bishop, Wilson lived some centuries too late. It is very difficult for us today to understand how an infinitely kind man like Bishop Wilson could have committed acts which seem to us tyrannical and barbarous. For offences which nowadays would not be punished at all, or at all events not punished severely, people were obliged to stand in church clothed in a white sheet, and to acknowledge their repentance before the congregation, or to stand in the market place with a horse's bit in the mouth and a bridle over the head. Wicked, but half-witted women were dragged behind a boat through the sea, and the owners of the boats were sent to prison if they refused to carry out this sentence. Yet the bishop cared passionately for the souls of his people, and believed that punishment of this kind was a way of leading into right ways of life.

No doubt to some extent he was helped in carrying out his policy by the fact that many of the Manx of those days were very superstitious and ignorant; but certainly many of his own ideas were out of date, and the task which he set himself was doomed to failure. At the end of his life, the church discipline which he had fought so hard to revive and maintain was decidedly weaker than he had found it, and the same causes which had led to its earlier abandonment elsewhere, were soon to bring about its final disappearance in the Island.

REFERENCES

Bishop Barrow's Deed, *Journal of Manx Museum*, II (1932), also, The Story of Castletown Grammar School, *ibid*, III (1937), pp. 242-245.

QUAYLE, J. R., Coinage of the Isle of Man, *ibid*, II (1931), pp. 14-16 (with illustrations).

SHERWOOD, R., *Manx Law Tenures*, Douglas, 1899.

Privy Council Appeal Cases, IV (1878-9), pp. 294-305.

FARRANT, R. D., *Mann, Its Land Tenure, Constitution, Lords Rent and Deemsters*, Oxford Press, 1937.

MOORE, A. W., *History*, II, 871-909; I, 486-523.

Chapter X.

THE ATHOLLS, AND THE SALE OF THE ISLAND

The Duke of Atholl Becomes Lord of Man

The tenth Earl of Derby left no children, and he was succeeded in the earldom by a distant cousin, Edward Stanley. On the other hand, under the terms of the grant made by James I, the lordship of Man passed to the second Duke of Atholl, James Murray, who was descended from a daughter of the seventh Earl of Derby. The Atholl dynasty in Man lasted less than thirty years, for the third Duke sold the lordship to the British Crown in 1765. Yet the Atholl family maintained its association with the Island for sixty years longer, since the fourth Duke possessed extensive rights as a landowner, and he was appointed governor-general in 1793.

James, Duke of Atholl, who succeeded to the lordship in 1736, signalised his accession by coming to the Island in person and presiding at the annual Tynwald. He was given an official welcome, for the people had grown very weary of the rule of the Derbys. Crowds of spectators cheered and waved their hats in the air, while the soldiers and militia saluted by firing a volley.*

There was more than pageantry in this visit, for the Duke played a personal part in the passing of some much needed reforms. The chief of these were embodied in an Act of Tynwald, passed in 1737, and christened the Manx 'Bill of Rights,' which assured to every one the right of trial by jury. It also declared that the customs duties, which had hitherto been levied on the sole authority of the lord, should in future be fixed only with the consent of the Keys, and of the Council and Deemsters.

The Sale of the Island

The Duke died in 1764, and was succeeded by his son-in-law, John, the third Duke, whose reign was destined to be very short. The British authorities had for some time been considering how best to stop the illicit trade which had become so serious in the Island. The growth of smuggling, as this illicit trade is

*For a description of Tynwald Day, 1736, see *Journal of the Manx Musuem*, V (1945-6), 171.

usually called, will be dealt with more fully in the next chapter, and for the moment it is sufficient to say that Man had become the centre of a vast network, as a result of which the British government was being deprived of large sums that should have been paid as customs duties. The traffic had reached such enormous proportions that it was estimated to be worth as high as a third of a million pounds annually. The remedy which finally suggested itself was that the king of England should again become the sovereign of the Island, with the right to fix the Manx customs duties and to appoint officers to collect them. To effect this, it was necessary to buy the sovereign rights from the lord. Thus, the Manx people would be taxed without having the right to decide what the taxes should be, but exactly the same thing was being done with the American colonies. This was the period which saw the outbreak of rebellion in North America, and the foundation of the United States; and the great statesman, Edmund Burke, in one of his famous speeches, compares the results of the British government's conduct in the Isle of Man and in America.

The Revesting and Mischief Acts (1765)

Shortly after his accession, the third Duke of Atholl was asked to state the sum for which he would sell his rights. He demanded time to consider the question, but was told plainly that steps would be taken to compel him to sell. The sum of £70,000 was decided on, and the agreement was put into effect by a measure of the British Parliament called the Isle of Man Revesting Act. This meant that the sovereignty of the Island, which the king of England had granted to Sir John Stanley in 1405, was now vested in the king once more. The bargain did not cover the duke's rights as lord of the manor, the most important of these being the ownership of the minerals, the 'boon' services from the tenants, and the appointment of the bishop and many of the clergy. The sum of £70,000 did, on the other hand, include the customs duties of the Island, which were henceforth transferred to the British government.

Just before this, Parliament passed a measure, usually called the Mischief Act, whose object was to stamp out the 'mischief of smuggling.' It gave power to the English customs officers to come into Manx ports and search suspected vessels, and laid it down that any offence against the revenue which had been committed in Man could be tried in the courts of Britain and Ireland. Manx merchants were prohibited from obtaining dutiable goods from foreign countries until they had been imported into England; and later, the British government only allowed such goods to reach the Isle of Man in limited quantities, with the result that the few persons who received the licences to import were able to charge what prices they chose. By another Act of the same year actual Manx produce was allowed, with certain exceptions, to be imported into Great Britain free of duty.

The Island under British Rule (1765-1793)

These drastic changes in their constitution came upon the Manx people as a humiliation and a disaster. Their ancient kingdom was destroyed by a bargain made over their heads. Although the House of Keys and the Legislative Council remained, the only power they had was to do things which did not cost money. The British government paid the expenses of administration, and kept any surplus taxation under its own control. At first this surplus was paid into a separate account, and there was an undertaking that it would be spent for the Island's benefit; but after a while it went straight into the revenue of the United Kingdom, and the government denied that the Isle of Man had any claim upon it. The officials sent to collect the customs duties regarded the Island as a nest of smugglers, and they treated the Manx with suspicion and disdain.

The smuggling trade had been so extraordinarily profitable that Manxmen had largely lost interest in fishing and farming. They had to rebuild these and other native industries, and in the meantime they suffered great loss. There was a panic among the owners of houses and warehouses, which could not be let or sold for as much as previously; merchants from Liverpool and Glasgow hastily left the Island, and the bold seafaring men who had earned their living by ' running ' cargoes from Douglas to the adjoining coasts had to look for other occupations.

In one respect the Island was almost immediately the better for the Act of Revestment. Its leading men came into closer contact with the British government officials and realised that some of the Manx laws were out of date. In 1777, Tynwald repealed the oppressive statutes which forced workmen to take employment in certain places and at certain rates of wages, and which enabled deemsters and other officials to obtain labourers and maidservants compulsorily by 'yarding.'

The Fourth Duke of Atholl as Governor-General (1793-1830)

The third Duke of Atholl died in 1774, and his son, who had had, of course, no share in making the bargain with the government, immediately began to claim that the sum paid was not enough. The Keys vigorously resisted the Duke's demands, and also passed laws obstructing the Duke in the collection of his manorial dues such as the custom on herrings, and the right of free labour on the Duke's houses. The British government repeatedly refused to increase the sum paid for the Duke's rights, but in 1793 they gratified him by appointing him the Island's governor-general. This gave him the power to superintend the administration of the Island, and he came over from time to time, and built as his Manx residence the splendid mansion overlooking Douglas Bay which is now the Castle Mona Hotel (Fig. 40). But there were still lieutenant-governors who carried out the work in detail.

The Duke's office enabled him to appoint some of the lesser officials himself, while his closer contact with the Manx people enabled him to win a measure of support amongst them. He continued to press his claims in London, and he had as 'friend at court' no less a person than the great William Pitt. Although the government's legal advisers had reported that the Duke's claims were unjustified, Pitt's authority was great enough to enable him, in 1805, to persuade a reluctant Parliament to pass an Act granting the Duke £3,000 a year, to come out of the Island's revenues. This grant was opposed by the House of Keys; and John Christian Curwen, a member both of the Keys and the House of Commons, made an eloquent speech in the latter chamber. In opposing the grant in the House of Lords, Lord Ellenborough, the Chief Justice of England at the time condemned the whole transaction as 'one of the most corrupt jobs ever witnessed in Parliament.'

The Duke's Relations with The People

Although always opposed by the Keys, the Duke was for a time a favourite with the people. The Keys were all men of property, and, as farmers, their interest was to keep the price of corn high so that they tried to prevent the import of corn even when it was scarce in the Island. On one occasion the Duke promised the people that they would not starve while he had a loaf. As to the Keys, he once told them that 'they were no more representatives of the people of Man than of the people of Peru.' There was a certain element of truth in this description when it is considered that the Keys were, at the time, a self-elected body. The Duke also used his influence with the government to stop the press-gangs from taking Manx fishermen to serve in the Navy; and in various ways, despite his restless ambition, the Island's interests were better looked after by him than by the British officials.

What Manxmen could not endure was the increasing presence of the Duke's Scottish dependents in various paid offices, and the limit was reached when he appointed his nephew, George Murray, as bishop. Bishop Murray demanded tithe on potatoes and other green crops which had gone free for many years. The farmers refused to pay, and riots broke out. The bishop was confronted in his own palace by a mob which called upon him to give up his claim, and he believed he was in danger of his life. He found it prudent to comply, and shortly afterwards he was given another bishopric, and so left the Island in 1827.

Final Settlement of the Atholl Claim

By this time the Duke was tired of the Isle of Man, and everyone was tired of the agitation over his claims. The British government offered to buy out the remainder of his rights, and, in 1828, they were purchased for £417,000. He continued to be governor-general until his death in 1830, but his last visit to the Island was in 1826.

In all, Great Britain paid about half a million pounds for the financial control of the Isle of Man, and, judged by the values of those times, the sum was most excessive. Yet in the hundred years during which they collected the Island's revenues, the British government gained a surplus greater than the total paid to the Duke, and, in addition, they earned good interest on the price of the crown lands and the royalties on the mines. The real sufferers from the deal were the Manx people, whose money was taken from them in taxation while public works, such as harbours, were for most of the time sadly neglected. A period of progress was to come—but it was not until a considerable time after the Atholls had left the Island.

REFERENCES

WALPOLE, SPENCER, *The Land of Home Rule*, 202-247, London, 1893.

MOORE, A. W., *History*, I, 384-391; II, 527-549.

An Abstract of the Laws, Customs and Ordinances of the Isle of Man, edited by James Gell, Manx Society, XII, Douglas, 1867.

CHAPTER XI

ECONOMIC AND SOCIAL CONDITIONS DURING THE 17TH AND 18TH CENTURIES

TRADERS AND SMUGGLERS

'THIS Isle will never flourish until some trading be.' This remark in a letter of the seventh Earl of Derby, written about 1643, gives some indication that in his time Manx trade was very small.

Ever since the arrival of the Stanleys, trade had been regulated in the primitive and thorough manner which was possible in so small an island. No goods could be taken out, and none brought in and distributed, without the permission of the lord. Customs duties were levied on all imports and exports.* Various officers were appointed to see that these rules were enforced, and the most interesting were the 'four merchants' whose business it was to bargain with the merchant stranger on behalf of the lord and the country.

The system of watch and ward (see p. 91) enabled the authorities to know whenever a ship was about to reach land. On the ship's arrival in port its master had to go in person before the governor, to declare the nature of his cargo, and also to tell him the latest news. After this he was taken in hand by the four merchants, whose duty it was to make the best bargain they could with him. The receivers of Castle Rushen and Peel Castle had the first choice in securing what they needed for those places, and afterwards the four merchants disposed of the remainder in the various parts of the Island. In one of the early orders it is directed that if the cargo consisted of wine, the clerk of the ships was allowed to bargain for one choice hogshead for himself, but, with this exception, no one was to have choice of wine 'but my lord, the captain (i.e. the governor), bishop, abbot or archdeacon and to drink it free of cost.'

No one was allowed to send goods out of the country until the governor had decided with the council what could be spared. The stranger buying commodities for export was forbidden to obtain them except in the public markets; and laws were

*There were no duties on *exports* after 1737.

enacted in the time of the seventh Earl against what we should call middlemen. It will be evident that such restrictions would not tend to encourage trade, but rather to stifle it. There was very little money in circulation, and for a long time most of the trade, both internal and external, had to be carried on by barter. The Island was badly in need of salt, iron, timber, tar, coal (though it produced its own fuel in the form of turf), besides all of the luxuries. Until the development of lead and silver mining, the Manx had nothing to export except the products of agriculture and the fisheries. Indeed, the external trade between 1660 and 1700 was so little that the customs duties on exports and imports combined produced less than £100 annually. During the eighteenth century the amount increased very considerably so that by 1750 the annual value was £3,500 or more.*

Conditions improved after the defeat of King Charles I, when many royalist refugees sought refuge in Man and brought with them a quantity of new money. Later, as has been stated, copper coins were minted in the Island, replacing the base currency in which traders could have no confidence. Instead of being confined to the Manx coast, fishermen ventured to Scotland and England to market their goods abroad, and trading vessels also began to disregard the old restrictions.

Manxmen have a well-marked aptitude for a life of sea-faring and maritime commerce, but unfortunately during the greater part of this period they were hampered by many restrictions imposed not only by their own government but also by the governments of surrounding lands. Normal trade with England was practically impossible since it was laid down in the Navigation Acts that goods could only be brought into that country by English-built and English-manned ships. Moreover, the English tariff was so heavy, especially after 1689, that any trading intercourse between the two countries became prohibitive.

Tynwald complained of this in a petition to Lord Derby in 1705, in which they pointed out that it was impossible for them to get the chief articles they required, including those indicated

*According to inquiries made by British Treasury officials in 1759 the income from the Insular customs was £6,000. See, Illicit trade with the Isle of Man, 1671-1765, R. C. Jarvis, in Trans. of Lancs. and Chesh. Antiq. Soc. (1945-46), 58.

above, unless they were able to export such articles as they could spare, and that they were prevented from doing this by the high English tariff. This appeal produced no result.

Under such conditions it is not surprising that towards the end of the seventeenth century, smuggling, or as it was called, the 'running trade' became a tempting enterprise and a thrilling adventure. Wines and spirits, tea, tobacco and other commodities could be brought from abroad, particularly France, Spain, Portugal, Norway and Sweden, landed at the Manx ports on payment of the comparatively small local duty, and run across to creeks and small bays on the coasts of England, Scotland, or Ireland. Smaller boats were specially built in such a style as to give them speed when dodging or flying from the revenue cutters, and also to enable them to run in to the Lancashire and other coasts, preferably at dusk, at a state of tide when deeper-draught vessels could not follow.

Conditions were, of course, such as to encourage similar activities round most of the English coasts, particularly in the south and east where investigations in the second half of the eighteenth century disclosed an amazing and bewildering state of affairs. But the Island's position, both strategically and constitutionally, helped to make it 'the very citadel of smuggling,' as Edmund Burke described it in his speech on American taxation in 1774. Merchants from surrounding countries, particularly England and Scotland, came to invest their capital in this new and promising business.* Gone were the old ideas of keeping 'strangers' at arm's length; the law was altered so as to place them in almost as good a position for trading as the native Manxmen. Manx ports, especially Douglas, were busy with fine ships carrying cargoes of the most desired goods in the world. The more the trade grew, the greater were the customs duties paid in the Island, and the lord and his officials made only a pretence of discouraging such trade.

*It should indeed be stressed that amongst the chief 'smugglers' were not merely those who carried the goods across the seas, but also the merchants who traded in them, in Man and in England; and most of these traders were of English or Scottish origin. On purely legal grounds it could be argued from the Manx standpoint that the trade was legitimate in so far as it did not violate Insular laws. The British authorities, on the other hand, condemned the trade as 'illicit and clandestine.' See, *Abstract of the Laws . . . of the Isle of Man*, Manx Soc., XII, p. 105. For some indication of conditions in England see, A. L. Cross, *Eighteenth Century Documents relating to the Royal Forests and Smuggling*, Ann Arbor, 1928.

The British government officials had no desire to be defrauded. They autocratically threatened to take steps for raising the Manx duties to the same level as those in Britain; they stationed their own officers in the Island to watch over their interests; they passed a law prohibiting the importation of foreign goods into Man for the purpose of being re-exported into Britain. An agreement was made whereby the Island was to pass that legislation for itself, provided that England withdrew the duties upon goods which were the home-grown products of the Island. Parliament did not keep its promise, and Tynwald did not consider itself bound either. Thereupon Parliament passed the Act over the Island's head, and later on, as described in the previous chapter, it regained by force the sovereignty of the Island. So by limiting the quantities of Manx imports, fixing the amounts of the duties and policing the Manx waters, it got what was called the 'smuggling mischief' under control.

How The People Lived

Little is known of the domestic and social life of the Manx before the period of the Commonwealth. In the year 1648 a Lancashire gentlemen, named William Blundell, 'wearied' as he says 'with being so often wakened at midnight to fly from the King's and Parliament's troops (both equally feared because equally plundering)' sought rest and refuge in Man. Other writers about the Island were Governor Chaloner, a late seventeenth century governor named William Sacheverell, and George Waldron, one of those English custom officers who had the 'mortification,' as he himself puts it, of seeing a 'stately cargo of indigo, mastic, raisins of the sun and other very rich goods, sold to the traders of Douglas without the least duty being paid to His Majesty!'

Then, as now, there were four principal towns, Castletown, Douglas, Ramsey and Peel. Castletown was the capital and the place of the lord's residence; but Douglas had more trade and a rather larger population because of its better harbour. In Blundell's day Ramsey and Peel were scarcely bigger than villages, and Ramsey port had been washed away not long before by a great storm.

The gentry and well-to-do folk lived in the country, and their houses were substantial and well-built. They generally spoke English, and Blundell says they were very like the people of Lancashire and Cheshire, both in manner of speech and way of life. The houses of farmers and tradesmen usually had only one storey, and were thatched with straw. In Douglas and Castletown there were houses of two storeys, and even three, and a few were roofed with slate. In such houses there was a stone stairway outside, such as may still be seen in old-fashioned barns. The poorer people lived in small cottages built of stones bound with mud, or of turf-sods alone, sometimes thatched with straw, broom, or bent, but often covered simply with sods of turf. The thatch was held in position by twisted ropes made of straw, called *suggane*.

These cottages very often consisted of a single room, with a loft over one end of it. If a second room existed it was called a *cullee*, or parlour. The floor was generally of earth, with an open fireplace or hearth called a *chiollagh*, where there was a long chain called a *slouree*, which suspended the big pot over the fire (Fig. 42). Turf, ling and gorse were used as fuel, though the better class houses used a mixture of turf and coal. In these cottages, small as they were, large families were often reared.

Blundell says that in many places, besides the man and his wife and children, there were geese and ducks under the bed, cocks and hens overhead, and the cow and calf at the bed's foot. This, of course, is an overstatement, but it must not be forgotten that T. E. Brown, over two centuries later, could write in *Betsy Lee:*

> 'You know the way them houses is fixed
> With the pigs and the hens and the childher mixed.'

Even today almost exactly the same kind of thing can be seen in parts of Ireland.

The food of the poorer classes consisted chiefly of herrings and oatcakes, while their drink was water or buttermilk, with beer (*jough*) on feast days and market days. When potatoes were introduced, they joined the herring to form the principal articles of Manx diet. These two are linked in the Christmas rhyme of good wishes, *Palchey phuddase as skeddan dy liooar* (potatoes in plenty and herring enough). The Island was not short of mutton, beef, bacon, poultry, eggs, honey or butter, but these were produced chiefly for sale.

Clothing was made from the wool of the native or *loaghtan* sheep, and from native-grown flax. The *loaghtan* wool, the natural colour of which is light-brown, has practically died out, but formerly it was much valued. Shoes and stockings were seldom worn either by men or women, except on Sundays. For work in the fields *carranes* were worn. They were untanned strips of cow-hide bound to the feet by thongs of the same material.

The native Manx horse was a small hardy beast with long black hair. Blundell says that a reasonably sized man needed no stirrup to mount one; but once mounted, the little animal would trot along all day and all night, needing very little to eat or drink. The cows are described as being small and poor. They lived in the open, summer and winter. When fodder became scarce, they were often fed on bruised gorse shoots, and most upland farms had a gorse mill for this purpose. When near the seashore they would feed on dulse and other seaweeds. According to Blundell cattle got to like this diet better than hay or grass, and throve better, and gave more milk on it; but with all respect to that writer, this is hard to believe, and he was probably trying to impress his English readers with the wonders of what was then a little known Island!

Down to the second half of the eighteenth century there were no wheeled carriages, sleds being used, and the roads were little better than bridle paths. Travel was mostly on foot or horseback; and goods were conveyed on panniers on the backs of horses or donkeys. Prices generally were very low. A goose could be bought for fourpence, and eggs ten or twelve for a penny.

Fairs were held very frequently throughout the parishes and the writers tell of two great national fairs—Midsummer, when the laws were proclaimed at St. John's (Fig. 49), and Michaelmas, held near the church of Kirk Michael. Allhallowtide (now called Hollantide), when the farm servants entered their new employment, was also an occasion of importance, and a fair was held on that day at Douglas. These three fairs still exist, and at the last two there is some hiring of servants, but they have fallen greatly into disuse. Women servants were hired on Lady Day, and until about twenty-five years ago a 'Ladies' Fair' was held in Sulby Claddagh, though no longer on Lady Day.

Though the Manx impressed their outside observers as being serious and even melancholy, they could amuse themselves on occasion. The young men had skill with bows and arrows, and archery matches were frequent. They also played a kind of hockey called *cammag*, which was exceedingly popular, and which was played until very recently. Dancing to the music of the fiddle and the bass viol was their favourite pastime, and they practised it in the fields in summer and the barns in winter.

Except for the upper classes and the shopkeepers in the towns, Manx was the common speech. There were no books in that language until Bishop Wilson published a Catechism in 1707, and set on foot the translation of the Scriptures. When people were taught to read, they could only learn to read English; any other teaching must have been by word of mouth. Most of the schools were carried on by the clergymen, though there were a few licensed schoolmasters; and in the early part of the nineteenth century, as may be gathered from the poems of T. E. Brown, the schoolmaster was often a tailor who went on sewing after he had set the children their tasks. Teaching was also considered an occupation suitable for a cripple.

Manxmen are always interested to learn what other people think of them. English writers say that they were shy and reserved with strangers, though friendly enough on a longer acquaintance, and that they were extremely frugal. The men were tall and 'of strenuous bulk,' and though full of mettle they were patient and law-abiding and loth to resist when oppressed. The women were active and lively, and much more industrious than the men. While the men were fishing it was the women who performed much of the labour in the fields and on the farm.

The people were at the same time deeply religious and highly superstitious. Unconscious of any inconsistency, they would offer prayers to Christ and St. Patrick, and would leave gifts to keep themselves on good terms with the fairies. The 'fairy doctor,' the 'wise woman' and the seller of charms were often resorted to.

The national character was greatly injured by the advent of smuggling, and the consequent cheapness and abundance of intoxicating liquors. Drunkenness became the Island's besetting sin. Colonel Richard Townley, who visited Douglas at the end of the eighteenth century, gives the Manx fishermen a bad character, and says that after a good period of fishing they would neglect their industry while they spent their profits on drinking. Seventy years earlier, Waldron wrote that the only diversion of the better sort of people was drinking. When people settled down to a quieter but more honest form of livelihood, when liquor became less plentiful, and when the Legislature took steps to regulate the number of alehouses, the Manx gradually returned to sobriety. They were helped in this by the reforming influence of the Methodists and a fine group of clergymen, and by the Rechabite and other temperance societies.

REFERENCES

Stanley Legislation of Man, Manx Society, III, Douglas, 1860.

BLUNDELL, WILLIAM, *A History of the Isle of Man,* Manx Society, 2 Vols. Douglas, 1875 and 1877.

MOORE, A. W., *History,* I, 392-460, also *Manx Worthies.*

WILLIAMSON, K., Characteristics of the *Chiollagh*, *Journal of the Manx Museum*, IV (1939), 25-28 (with illustrations).

DOUGLAS, MONA, The Traditional Dances of Man, *ibid*, V (1941), 3-7 (with illustrations).

CRAINE, DAVID, Sorcery and Witchcraft in Man, *ibid*, IV (1939) 122-124.

Household Prices 160 years ago, *ibid.* IV (1939), 36, 65 and 85.

The Four Merchants, *ibid*, II (1934), 185.

KNEEN, J. J., Manx Fairs and Festivals, Pagan and Christian. *Proc. I.M. Nat. Hist. and Antiq. Soc.* III, 36-82.

An Abstract of the Laws, Customs and Ordinances of the Isle of Man, edited by James Gell, Manx Soc., XII, Douglas, 1867.

Chapter XII.

THE MANX CHURCH AND THE RISE OF METHODISM

Developments in the Church—The Manx Bible

Bishop Wilson was followed by the equally good, though not equally great, Bishop Mark Hildesley (1755-1772). Hildesley's lovable disposition is shown in numerous letters to friends in the Island and in England, which are delightful in their wit, their wisdom, and their kindliness. If Bishop Wilson was born to command, then Hildesley was born to be an elder brother.

He plunged with enthusiasm into the work involved in the publication of the Manx Bible. Most of this was printed in his time, besides the Prayer Book and some religious works; and before he died he had the happiness of seeing the last printed pages of the translation of the Bible. The task was divided among the parish clergymen, their work being revised by the Rev. Philip Moore the headmaster of the Douglas Grammar School, and his pupil John Kelly. In some passages the Manx Bible differs from the English, since Philip Moore made use of the results of the learning which had been made available since the English translation in 1611. The Manx translation is considered a very good one, and, in the words of one writer, 'the beautiful expression of the Manx, superior to the Irish translation, is visible to every Celtic scholar.'

Once when John Kelly was bringing a batch of the manuscript to Whitehaven to be printed, his ship was wrecked, and the precious papers were saved through Kelly holding them out of reach of the water for five hours.

Bishop Hildesley was less successful in his endeavour to keep alive his predecessor's system of ecclesiastical discipline. He found that the churches were not large enough to hold the population, so that he caused some to be rebuilt, and added one or two new ones. St. Mark's Church, Malew, is the work of Bishop Hildesley, and St. George's, Douglas, was begun in his time.

Another great church-builder was Bishop Ward, who held the see from 1828 to 1838. He raised large sums of money in England for the replacement and increase of churches in the Island. St. Barnabas', Douglas, and St. Luke's, Baldwin, were founded by him. By the same appeal to English friends and sympathisers, mainly through the efforts of Rev. Hugh Stowell, Rector of Ballaugh, he greatly increased the funds of the Bishop Barrow Charity, and a dream of over two centuries was made real by the opening of King William's College in 1833. The education given there is similar to that in the important English public schools, and it is provided for boys living both within and outside the Island. In the past few years, especially since the Legislature helped to find money for modernising the school buildings, King William's College has been linked more closely with the whole Manx educational system (Fig. 41). Bishop Ward also played a major role in resisting a strong attempt made in 1836 to abolish the independent bishopric of Sodor and Man and to unite it to that of Carlisle. As a result of the opposition which was organised, the scheme was finally defeated, and the Manx diocese continued to exist as a separate see.

Other educational activities during this period included the establishment of a new school in Peel, as a result of the efforts of Bishop Hildesley, and also what was called the Lancasterian school in Athol Street, Douglas.

By an Act of Tynwald passed in 1839, the church got rid of the long quarrel over the tithes. By the end of the eighteenth century the tithe on herrings and other fish, about which there had been a long controversy, ceased to be paid, and Bishop Murray's ill-fated attempt to collect the tithe on potatoes has already been referred to. The method of collecting the tithes also gave rise to disturbances, and it became clear that the payment of a definite money charge, rising or falling each year according to the English market price of grain, was much preferable to that of paying in kind. The Tithe Commutation Act of 1938, which made the money payment possible, not only improved the position of the Manx clergy, but it made less likely any friction between them and the tithe-payers.

The Apostles of Methodism

The first Methodist preacher in the Island was John Murlin, sometimes nicknamed 'the weeping prophet.' He visited Ramsey in 1758, and declared that the Isle of Man was a nest of smugglers and that he could do no good there. Eighteen years later John Crook came from Liverpool and ultimately met with success. At first he had to face opposition and even violence, for in Douglas he was attacked by a mob, who thought they had the support of the minister of St. Matthew's. Bishop Richmond, a haughty overbearing man, issued a letter to his clergy violently condemning the Methodists, but the Governor was very friendly, and some of the clergymen gave the movement their approval.

John Wesley himself visited Man in 1777 and 1781. The membership of the 'Society,' as it was then called, became very great, and Wesley was delighted with the earnestness of the local preachers and the singing of the congregations. 'The local preachers are men of faith and love, knit together in one mind and one judgment,' he wrote in his Journal, where he also stated 'I have never heard better singing either in Bristol or London . . . What has been seen like it (the growth of the Society) in any part either of Great Britain or Ireland?'

The Wesleyan Methodists were followed by the Primitive Methodists, who established themselves in the Island in 1823 after the arrival of John Butcher, a preacher from Bolton, who landed from a fishing boat at Derbyhaven.

The Manx Bible was succeeded at no great interval by a Manx hymn-book (1795), published for the Methodists. About the same period there was being composed a mass of religious verse, under the general title of *carvals* or carols, which is almost the only kind of original literature in the Manx language.

Manx Methodism

Methodism has a great hold on the Manx people today, but it has caused little serious disagreement with the established Church. The Island has indeed been fortunate in having been spared not only the mutual persecution of Protestants and Roman Catholics during the period of the Reformation, but also the repression of Dissenters which was practised in England particularly during the seventeenth century. On the contrary, for long after the coming of Methodism, people would go to the church in the morning and the chapel at night, and the parish clerk might be a local preacher. To this day some of the church-wardens are active Methodists. Legislation has been obtained which enables Nonconformists to have baptisms, marriages and funerals performed in their own churches; but a good many

Methodists have such an attachment to the parish church that they do not think of exercising their liberty. Religious differences sometimes have an influence in elections to the House of Keys. As a rule, however, Churchmen and Methodists live happily together; and a notable feature of the present day in, at any rate, one parish are the united services held, for example, in support of the Island's hospitals.

Wesleyan Methodists and Primitive Methodists have been known to be suspicious of each other, with separate chapels in some districts, but the union of the Methodist churches which came into effect some years ago is expected, in Man as in other places, to cause these disagreements to pass away.

There is much evidence that in the eighteenth century England was sinking into irreligion and looseness of life, and that it was helped in raising itself by the virtue and zeal of the Methodists. In the Island, similar evils were calling for a similar remedy. The smuggling trade had made a number of the people somewhat reckless and drunken. Methodism, happily, with its strong personal appeal, together with its insistence on temperance, proved an immense power for good in winning the people back to better ways of life. An emotional form of worship like early Methodism may have its dangers, but it filled men and women first with fear and then with a glowing hope. Moreover, it reached those who had been unaffected by the orderliness and the serene beauty in the Book of Common Prayer. What is most genuine in Methodism and in the historic Episcopal Church have united to create all that we like to think of as typical and representative in the Manx character.

REFERENCES

BUTLER, WEEDON, *Memoirs of Bishop Hildesley*, London, 1799. *The Letters of Bishop Hildesley*, Douglas, 1904.

ROSSER, J., *History of the Wesleyan Methodism in the Isle of Man*, 1869.

CUBBON, W., The Scriptures, Carvals, etc., in the Manx Language; in, *Bibliography of the Literature of the Isle of Man*, II, pp. 749-836, London, 1939.

MOORE, A. W., *History*, II, 652-681, also, *Diocese of Sodor and Man*, S.P.C.K., London, 1893.

Chapter XIII.

THE REFORM OF THE KEYS AND THE PARTIAL RESTORATION OF FINANCIAL CONTROL (1866)

Conditions During the Early Nineteenth Century

Gradually the Island recovered from the turmoil and the setback caused by the abolition of the smuggling traffic. Improved methods were introduced into agriculture, and there were many seasons of prosperity among the fishermen. In the later eighteenth and early nineteenth centuries, great quantities of red and white herrings were exported to British as well as to French, Spanish and Italian ports, and even to America. (Figs. 43 and 44). The customs duties were considerably lower than in England, and people who lived on comparatively small fixed incomes found that a sum which would barely maintain them in England or Ireland would, in the Island, enable them to live comfortably. Their number was increased at the end of the wars with Napoleon, when many army and navy officers were retired upon half-pay.

There was another, and much less respectable, class of immigrants into the Island. People who owed money in England, and were, under the laws of that period, liable to be imprisoned until they had paid their debt, could not be pursued by their creditors into Man. Some of them were dishonest, and brought with them considerable sums of money with which, when in the Island, they usually paid their way. Their purchases were of benefit to the Manx tradesmen, and laws were passed for their protection. The tradesmen were in turn protected against them by laws which allowed him, if he suspected they were about to leave the Island, to have them arrested and detained until they paid, or gave security for what they owed. The presence of such absconding debtors tended to give the Island a bad reputation; but, after a while, the laws were modified and Man ceased to be regarded as a refuge for the shiftless and the dishonest Englishman.

Residents in England began to visit the Island in the summer for the sake of what was then called the 'sea bathing,' and

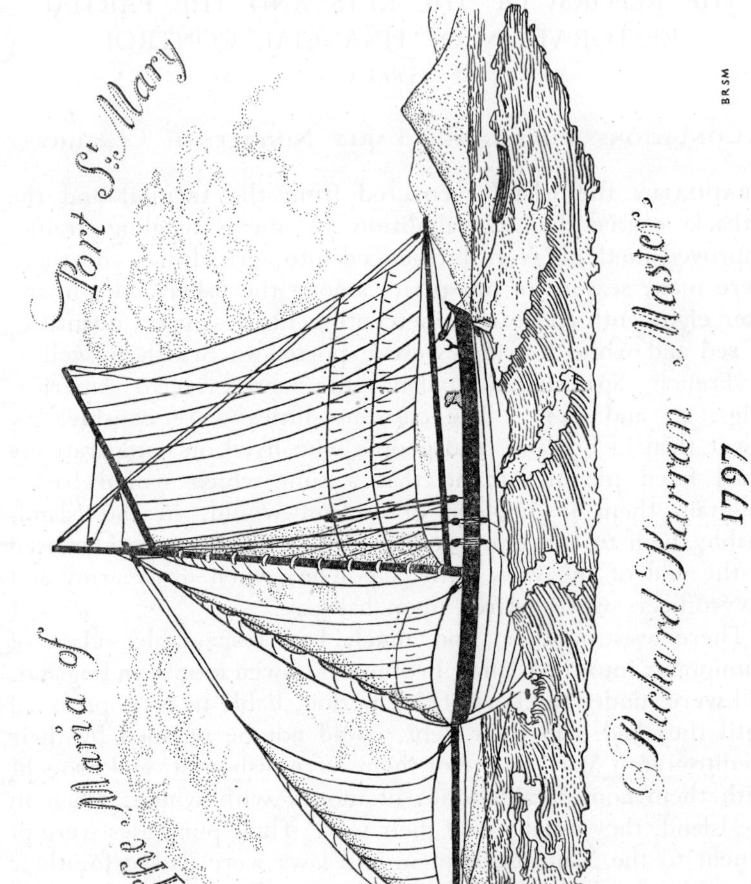

Fig. 43.—An eighteenth century smack (after the original hand-painted design on a handsome oval dish of white china)

communications became easier, quicker, and more regular after the establishment of a passenger steamer service between Douglas and Liverpool in 1829. The political union of the Island with Britain entitled Manx ships to be regarded as British ships, and to get their share of the British carrying trade.

Beginnings of The Reform Movement

After 1796, the receipts from Manx customs duties grew so much that they exceeded the amount spent on the Island's government, and left the British government with substantial surpluses for several years. On the other hand the British authorities paid little attention to the growth of the Island's population, or to the need for better harbours which followed from the increase in trade. For half a century the Manx were agitating for the right to handle their own revenues, so that they could provide harbours and other national necessities, instead of having to wait until the British government could be made interested in the subject.

Side by side with this patriotic movement for self-government there was a democratic movement, for government by the people. As early as 1780 a petition was prepared for submission to Parliament, and was signed by 800 inhabitants, urging that the House of Keys might be dissolved and replaced by a body chosen at regular periods by popular election. The Keys declared that this petition was organised on behalf of the Duke of Atholl, in order to undermine their influence when fighting for what were the people's rights; and it could have been said in their favour that, in a rough and ready way, they represented the same classes of the population as had any real representation in the Parliament of England at the same time.

In 1832 Parliament passed the celebrated Reform Bill, which went a long way towards making the choice of government the genuine privilege of the mass of the people. A reform party newspaper, the *Mona's Herald*, was established in the Island in the following year, and the battle for popular government became increasingly keen. At first the British authorities told the agitators that if any reform was decided upon, it might consist of giving the Manx one elected representative in the House of Commons, and bringing the Island's separate government to an end. Later, they told Tynwald that they could not hand the control of taxes paid by the people to a body whom the people had not chosen.

Reform of The Keys

Such was the state of affairs when Henry Brougham Loch (later, Lord Loch) became governor in 1863. Soon after his appointment he came to the conclusion that the Island's future prosperity depended upon developing trade and the holiday traffic, and that the Manx government must obtain power to raise and spend money on harbours. As that power, he declared, could only be obtained on condition that the House of Keys was reformed, the self-elected House must vote itself out of existence. The house was ill-advised, in the meantime, to imprison the editor of a Douglas newspaper for criticisms passed upon it, with the result that an English tribunal, the Privy Council, quashed the sentence and the Isle of Man Common Law Court ordered the House to pay the editor compensation. The two problems, namely, the reform of the Keys and the question of financial control, were settled together in 1866, when an Isle of Man Customs and Harbours Act was passed by Parliament, and a House of Keys Election Act was passed by Tynwald.

Since that date the Island has levied its own taxes and spent its own moneys, except that the essential costs of government, such as the salaries of the governor and his staff, and the judges and police, are what are called 'reserved services.' The British government makes sure that these charges on the revenue are paid before anything else, and it will not let them be altered by anyone but itself. It was also provided that the Island should make an annual contribution of £10,000 to the British government. This sum was fixed upon as representing interest on the money which the government paid to the Dukes of Atholl, and some have argued that the Manx people ought not to be called upon to pay it. It has also been described as a payment for the Island's protection by the British armed forces, and it cannot be denied that such a contribution was reasonable. Since the first World War of 1914-1918 the contribution made by Man to the British government has been considerably increased, as will be seen in the final chapter.

The New House of Keys

For the purpose of elections to the House of Keys, the Island was divided into ten constituencies made up of the six sheadings with three members each, the town of Douglas with three members, and the towns of Ramsey, Peel, Castletown, with one member each. In time the population of Douglas increased while that of some of the sheadings became less, so in 1891 a Redistribution Act was passed, under which one member was taken from Michael and one from Garff; and Douglas was made into two electoral districts, of which the northern returned three members, and the southern, two. In recent years it has been claimed that the proportion of population has altered still more in favour of Douglas and against some of the sheadings, but there has not been any further change in the basis of representation.

Nowadays, every man and woman above the age of twenty-one has a vote in choosing the members of the House of Keys, and the members themselves are no longer bound to be owners of property. The only disqualification is that of being a clergyman of the Church of England in the actual charge of a parish. The first woman member was elected in 1933. Unmarried women and widows who owned property have had the right to vote since 1881, thirty-seven years before women were granted the franchise in England.

History of the Keys

To conclude this chapter it will be appropriate to give a summary of the chief stages in the history of the House of Keys. It has already been seen that in Norse times the Keys were a kind of jury, assisting the Deemsters when any question of doubt or difficulty arose, to declare the ancient customary or breast law. This was also their function at the beginning of the Stanley period, when records of the Keys really begin; but their meetings were by no means regular, nor were they regarded as a permanent body. This judicial aspect of their work persisted, and the Keys continued to act as the supreme Court of Appeal in the Island until the Act of 1866 finally abolished that side of their duties. It is not definitely known how the Keys were appointed in the early days of the Stanleys, except that in 1430, it is vaguely suggested that the 'twenty-four' were selected from thirty-six men, six being from each sheading in which they had been chosen by the whole commons.

From declaring the old laws, the function of the Keys passed in time to the making of new laws; but this development did not take place quickly, nor was it accomplished without a long struggle.

The first occasion on which the Keys are referred to as meeting with the two Deemsters to *enact* certain laws was in 1585. During the early seventeenth century, laws were made more frequently, and the Keys took part in making them, but the seventh Earl, the Great Stanley, did not wish this to be regarded as a definite right to do so.

After the Restoration, in 1660, the Keys lost much of their authority, for the high-handed eighth Earl removed seven members in 1662, because they were suspected of being favourable to *Illiam Dhone* who was then on trial; and he threatened a number of them in 1668, because they returned a verdict which challenged his ownership of the land. In 1677 he altered the customs rates without consulting them, and apparently dismissed nine members who had protested. This may be gathered from the fact that in a list of members of the House of Keys from the earliest times, which has been drawn up by Mr. Ramsey B. Moore, a former Attorney-General, nine new names appear in 1677. The customs duties were again altered without the Keys' consent in 1692. Promises were made that they would be consulted in the future, and they did take part in legislation connected with the customs in 1711 and 1714; but the principle that taxation could not be altered without the consent of the Keys was not definitely stated until 1737, in that great measure which has already been referred to as the Manx *Bill of Rights*.

With the Revestment came the definite loss of power, not merely by the Keys, but by Tynwald as a whole, and it was not until 1866 that the power was in some measure regained.

At what date the Keys came to be self-elected it is very difficult to say, although it is known that it was such a body in 1610, and that it had been so for at least a generation before that. When a member died, or ceased to hold office, the remainder nominated two persons of whom the governor selected one as his successor. It is, however, an interesting fact that in 1643 (and also in 1608) there is reference to 'four men of every parish' chosen by the people, who were consulted along with the Keys when any special matter was under discussion. They had apparently no power, but their existence reveals that the idea of popular election had, to some extent, survived. In 1866, the House of Keys became an elected body, and, owing to the popular support since given to it, it has acquired added strength so that it now occupies a vital and unchallenged role in the affairs of the Island.

REFERENCES

MOORE, A. W., *History*, II, 737-841.

WALPOLE, SPENCER, *Land of Home Rule*, 248-255.

MOORE, RAMSEY B., The Worthiest Men in the Land during five centuries, *Journal of the Manx Museum*, II, (1933), 143-147. (Contains names of the Keys from 1417).

Petition demanding popular election of Keys (1780), *ibid*, III, (1937), 195-201.

FARRANT, R. D., *Mann*, Ch. II, 28-52.

GILL, J. F., *Statutes of the Isle of Man*, I, London, 1883.

CUBBON, W., The Romance of the Brig Caesar, *Sea Breezes, The P.S.N.C. Magazine,* XX, (1936). 203-5, also, *Journal of the Manx Museum*, II, (1935), 63-65.

Chapter XIV.

CHIEF INDUSTRIES AND POPULATION

During its history the Island has had four main industries, namely, agriculture, fishing, mining, and catering for tourists or visitors, and it is interesting to see how these have influenced one another in the past, and at the present. In earlier days there was a very intimate connection between agriculture and fishing, many of the men being fishermen during the summer and farmers during the rest of the year. Similarly some of the miners of former days also engaged in fishing or in agriculture. Nowadays, farming and the visiting or tourist industry are left as the two great occupations, and the former is dependent for its development and success on the latter which is the dominating industry at the present.

Agriculture

Agriculture of some kind has been practised for about four thousand years in the Island, since it is now known that some form of wheat was being cultivated by the builders of the Meayl Circle, Cregneash, about 2,000 years B.C. Knowledge of Manx agriculture is, nevertheless, very scanty indeed until the seventeenth and eighteenth centuries; and it is not until the beginning of the nineteenth century that a systematic account of farming conditions over the Island is available, in the survey made by Thomas Quayle in 1812.

From descriptions given by this as well as by other writers, conditions appear to have been very primitive in many parts. Quayle speaks of Manx agriculture as being 'a recent art,' and complains that many farmers gave it little serious attention. There was not much attempt at a proper rotation of crops, the prevailing practice being to plough and raise corn crops, chiefly oats and barley, until the land became exhausted, when it would be allowed to lie in grass until it had recovered some of its fertility. It must be remembered that clover had only been introduced about 1770, while turnips were first cultivated here about 1780, so that it was only after that date that the existing five or six course rotation became possible. To illustrate how restricted the cultivation of turnips was during the early nineteenth century, it may be observed that in 1811 only about 600 acres of these roots were grown, whereas nowadays over 5,000 acres of turnips are produced each year. Many of the cattle and sheep at that period were of the original Manx breeds, and were small if hardy animals. They were being replaced by imported breeds, a process that has gone on steadily ever since. It is difficult to say how many cattle existed at that time, but in 1806 it was estimated that there were about 18,600 sheep in the whole Island, a small total compared with about 95,200 which existed in 1938.

The implements used by Manx farmers during the late eighteenth century were very primitive. Though threshing machines had just come into use, farm carts were almost unknown, the usual method of carriage being by creels on horses' backs, or by sleds, which were carts without wheels. Their ploughs, which were of a very rude make, and required two men to manage them, were drawn by teams of oxen or horses, the latter being preferred on the lowlands; and their harrows had teeth made of wood hardened over the fire, which had to be sharpened every morning before being used.

When Quayle wrote in 1812, Manx farms varied in size from about 10 to 150 acres, owned and cultivated by yeoman farmers, while there were probably not more than sixty farms consisting of 200 acres or more, each owned by one person. Fairly small farms have always been characteristic of Man, and at the present day practically 90 per cent of all the holdings are not more than 150 acres in extent, while about 28 per cent are between 50 acres and 100 acres, and 20 per cent between 20 and 50 acres in size. On the other hand, as compared with the early nineteenth century not so many holdings at the present day are worked by their owners, and indeed only about 30 per cent of the cultivated land is now occupied by owners, the remainder being occupied by tenant farmers.

The farms containing this cultivated land are found on the lowlands of the south-east and the north, as well as on the coastal plateaux on both sides of the Island, and now extend us the slopes of the hills to a height of about 600 feet. At the beginning of the nineteenth century cultivation extended for another hundred feet or so above its present limit; and while some of the higher land belonged to lower-lying farms, some of it was *intack* (or *intake*) land, held by smallholders or crofters who also engaged in fishing, or, in certain areas, in mining. With the decline of the other industries came the decay of these little homesteads; and the many *tholtans* or ruined cottages now remain as mute witnesses of the change that has taken place (See Fig. 1).

The long standing connection between farming and fishing which persisted until well into the nineteenth century, was condemned by agricultural writers such as Quayle, as well as by the authors of the various Reports to the Workington Agricultural Society in 1807 and 1808. In the 1807 Report, the writer considered that most of the persons employed were 'neither expert at fishing nor skilful cultivators of the earth,' while it was also pointed out that, owing to the fact that the herring-fishery clashed with the harvest, much of the field-labour at that period was performed by women. Since those days, the farmers have confined their energies to the work of cultivating the land, and the herring-fishery has steadily declined until it almost threatened to become extinct.

Nowadays, Manx agriculture is in a more flourishing condition than it was a hundred years or so ago, and it is primarily dependent on the all-important visiting industry. An interesting feature as compared with many other parts of the United Kingdom at the present day is the relatively high percentage of arable land. Of the total *cultivated* land in the Island, (excluding, of course, the heath or mountain land), almost 70 per cent was actually arable in 1939, leaving only 30 per cent under permanent grass. The corresponding figures for England and Wales were, arable 36 per cent and permanent pasture 64 per cent. In 1948 the proportion of arable was even still higher in Man, reaching 82 per cent, thus leaving only 18 per cent for permanent grass. By reference to Fig. 47 it will be seen that rough grazings (or mountain and heath land) have there been taken into account in working out the proportions of farmland in each parish and in the Island as a whole. On this basis the arable formed about 53 per cent of the farmland, rough grazings 27 per cent and permanent grass 20 per cent in 1939, while the respective figures for 1948 were 52 per cent, 37 per cent and 11 per cent.

Fig. 44.—The Brig *Caesar*, in the bay of Naples, 1788. Built at Douglas in 1783. Records exist of her voyages to Naples, Nice, etc., with red herrings bringing back wines and silks, and to the West Indies whence she returned with rum and sugar.

Fig. 45.—Port St. Mary—fishing boats in the Old Harbour, about 50 years ago

Fig. 46.—Foxdale Mines—a photograph taken about 1860

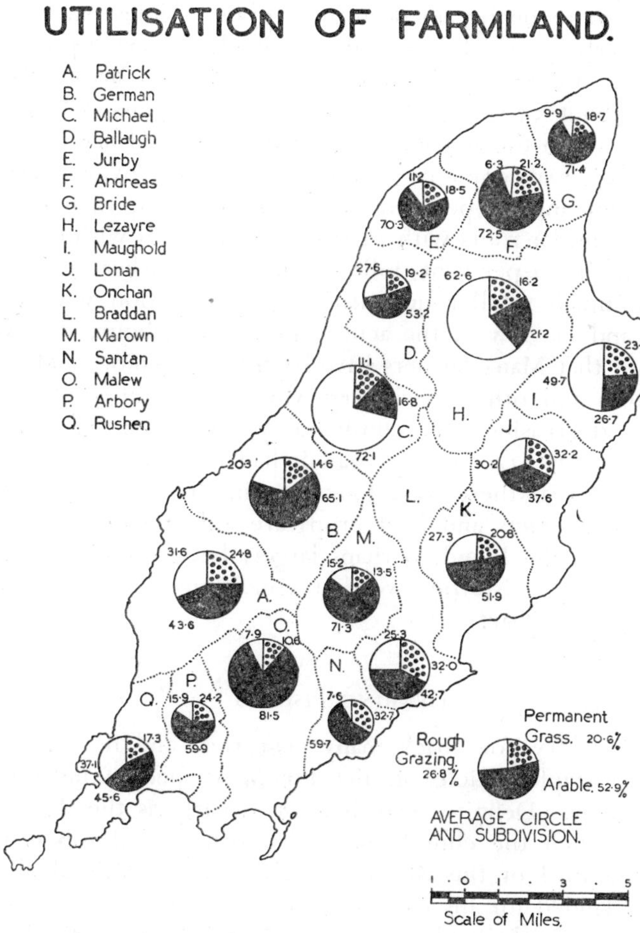

Fig. 47.—Each circle is proportional to the amount of farmland in the parish indicated. The sub-divisions of each circle show the percentages of the area in arable, permanent grass and rough grazing in the years before 1939. Note: the average figure for Rough Grazing should be 26.5%, not 26.8%.

In many ways these figures are an indication of the fact that Manx soils are very often of the leaner type, and not deep and rich enough to be left in permanent grass. Unless such lands are regularly worked they fairly quickly revert to a wild condition. Of the total arable area, by far the greatest proportion, about 55 per cent, is under rotation grass, which can be attributed to the seasonal demand for lamb and beef, as well as for milk. Oats come next in importance, occupying between 27 per cent and 28 per cent of the arable area, then turnips and other similar roots with 12 per cent, potatoes with between 2 per cent and 3 per cent, followed by barley, wheat and other crops in much smaller quantities. In connection with these figures, and in view of the acute shortage of labour, it is very significant that Manx farmers have been turning more and more to tractors and other machinery while the number of horses has been decreasing very considerably. In 1939 the number of tractors was 114, but by 1948 it had increased to 621, and in the same year there were four combine harvesters. Market-gardening products and fruit crops are unfortunately not well developed in the Island, perhaps largely because of the usually cold and very boisterous weather conditions during the early months of the year.

Herring Fishing

This industry goes back many centuries, and herrings have formed a staple article of diet for Manx people until quite recent times. Definite records exist as early as the thirteenth century, when the church claimed a tithe of all fish caught, while the lord of the Island also claimed one-fifth of all the herrings landed for his own use, as well as for the use of the garrisons at Castle Rushen and Peel Castle, (the Castle Mazes, as these supplies were called). All quarterland holders were compelled to provide themselves with nets, and the people were warned to keep their boats and nets in readiness for the fishing. After 1610, a water-bailiff was appointed to supervise the herring fleet and to see that all the various regulations were carried out. Herring fishing was not allowed to begin until the early part of July, a rule that was kept until the early nineteenth century, when boats from other parts of the British

Isles came to take part in the fisheries, and regulations were relaxed so that fishing began earlier.

Herring fishing was not a whole-time occupation for Manxmen since it only lasted normally during the four months July to October; and during the remainder of the year the men usually did farm work. Fishing operations were conducted off the western coast, beginning north of Peel, always the chief fishing port, and working south as the season advanced, so that in August, the principal month, the chief grounds were to the south-west of the Calf Island. At one time it was customary for the boats to move to the eastwards during the later part of the season to fish off Douglas in September and October; but this area was always very uncertain, and no serious fishing has been conducted there since 1918.

During the second half of the nineteenth century, it became the regular practice for many fishing boats to go to the mackerel fishery at Kinsale, in the south-east of Ireland, before the local herring fishing began. The boats went to Kinsale in March and returned in the middle of June. Then, with the close of the Manx fishing season, some boats followed the herrings along the west and north of Scotland, using as their base ports Stornaway, in the Island of Lewis, and Lerwick, in the Shetland Isles. This practice ceased during the early years of the present century.

In 1826, the Manx fishing fleet consisted of 250 boats totalling 7,000 tons, and employed 2,500 men, all natives of the Island. There were, in addition, about 300 vessels from Cornwall, Scotland, and Ireland which came to fish in Manx waters, while other boats were employed as carriers of fish for the English and Irish markets. After this there came a decline in the fishery, and the Manx fleet numbered only 200 in 1835. A revival came in the fifties, after which there was an increase not only in the number of vessels but also in their size, while their equipment, particularly as regards nets, was much improved. In 1864 the herring fishery employed nearly 300 boats and 2,800 men, and earned about £70,000 in the year. It should also be remembered that the additional trades of net-making, sailcloth-making and boat-building were maintained by the fishing industry. Since 1883 there has been a fairly steady decline, so that by 1914 the Manx herring fleet had dropped to 57, including 35 large boats, called *nickies*, about 50 feet long, and 22 smaller *nobbies* between 30 and 35 feet long (Fig. 45). Most of these were owned by Peel men, the remainder belonging to Port St. Mary.

Despite financial help from Tynwald, the Manx fleet had unfortunately dwindled by 1939 to only 9 vessels with crews totalling 47. These boats consisted of 4 motor-nobbies, 4 motor-boats built in 1937 for ring-net or drift-net, and one smaller motor-boat engaged in drifting for herrings and seine-netting for plaice. That this decline cannot be attributed, as is frequently suggested, to a falling off in the abundance of fish on the grounds is proved by the fact that boats from other ports are still attracted to the fishing in good numbers. In 1939, for example, there were 163 vessels from other ports, principally Scottish, although some came from East Anglia and some from Ireland. Of these other vessels taking part in the Manx herring fishing, 67 were motor-drifters, 64 steam-drifters and 32 ring-net boats. Hence the Manx vessels were responsible for only 11 per cent of the herrings landed during the last pre-war fishing season. One important factor which has contributed to this unhappy decline of Manx fishing is the high capital cost of the very specialised modern fishing vessels. An additional reason is to be found in the fact that, to the Manxman, fishing has never really been a whole time occupation as it is to his English or Scottish competitor, while in recent times the tourist industry has proved a more profitable alternative to fishing.

The returns for 1947 indicate that, on the whole, conditions were no worse than they were in 1939, but that there seemed to be distinct possibilities for development. Of the 10 Manx vessels engaged in 1947, with crews totalling 52, eight were new type motor boats. In all, these vessels accounted for no more than 9 per cent of the herrings caught on the local grounds; and of the total catch only 52 per cent went into the Manx market while the remainder was taken direct to the ports of Portpatrick, Holyhead and Ardglass (Co. Down).

As regards the disposal of the catch, it is known that herrings were cured in the Island two hundred years ago, since it was recorded in 1754 that 'everybody at Douglas is busy curing herrings . . . Upwards of 500 tons were salted in bulk at

Douglas, and shipped to Ireland, etc., besides some thousands of barrels cured for the West Indies.' Pickled herrings were exported to England and Ireland, and contributed a large part of the diet of the poorer people in many villages and inland towns.

The art of curing red herrings was introduced from Yarmouth in 1771, and the business increased in Man towards the end of the eighteenth century and continued to flourish until about 1830. Douglas was the main centre, having five large red herring houses in operation in 1815, but curing houses also existed at Port St. Mary and Derbyhaven.

The greater part of the catch was, however, taken by buying boats which received the herrings direct from the fishermen at sea; and the fish were then carried into the ports of the Island to be barrelled up or taken to such markets as Liverpool or Dublin. At Liverpool they were smoked for 'red' or packed for 'white' herrings according to the demand. This port was then actively engaged in the slave trade and exported large quantities of cured herrings to the West Indies where they formed an important part of the diet of the negroes. With the abolition of slavery in 1833 the consumption of herrings in the West Indies rapidly declined so that by 1840 the export trade both from Liverpool and the Isle of Man almost ceased.

From that date the Manx herring catch seems to have been disposed of mainly in a fresh state, and there are no records of curing operations of consequence until 1909 when the establishment of a curing station at Port St. Mary gave a great stimulus to the herring fishery at that port. Further stations were opened there and also at Douglas and Peel, and in the period between 1925 and 1939 pickle-curers took about 67 per cent of the total catch. Kipperers have also taken a fair proportion of the Manx catch for fifty years or so, and probably during the fifteen years ending in 1939 they accounted for about 30 per cent on the average.

Since then the positions of these two methods of disposal have been reversed, because in 1947 kipperers took 70 per cent of the total catch of herrings while pickle-curers took only 28 per cent. The future of the pickle-curing export trade, which was mainly to the continent of Europe, is still very uncertain, but kippers are consumed in the British Isles, and the outlook for the Manx kipper trade is much more promising granted that the quality of the article can be maintained.

Other Fisheries

Apart from herrings, other fisheries are carried on including the cod from Douglas and Port Erin, plaice from Peel, crab and lobster from Port Erin and Port St. Mary, and skate from Ramsey. All of these are now on a very reduced scale, having diminished rapidly like the herring fishery in recent times. In 1937 only a dozen men were engaged in cod fishing whereas in 1922, 151 were employed.

An interesting new fishery which only began a few years before the war was the dredging of escallops off Bradda Head. Good markets were found for the catch, particularly in the large English cities, and operations rapidly developed. During the six winter months from November 1937 to April 1938 the amount realised for the catch was practically £6,000, which was almost three times as much as Manx fishermen received for herrings during the summer fishery.

Mining

It is well known that ores of lead, (also containing silver), zinc, iron, and copper occur in veins throughout many portions of the Manx Slates, and mining operations have taken place in a number of centres in the past. Two areas have stood out as being of primary importance, namely Foxdale (producing lead and silver), and Laxey (producing lead, silver, and some copper), but old workings may be seen, for example, at Bradda Head, Ballacorkish, and Ballasherlogue, all for lead and silver in the parish of Rushen, at Langness (for copper) and at Maughold Head (for iron).

It is difficult to say how far back actual mining operations go, but there is documentary evidence that lead was obtained from Man in the thirteenth century for the roofing of castles built by Edward I in Wales. In the grant of the land to Sir John Stanley in 1405 'mines of lead and iron' are also mentioned. Passing to the period after the Restoration, we find that the search for minerals was carried out more systematically, much attention being devoted to coal which has never been found in Man.

The most prosperous period for mining came after the third and fourth decades of the nineteenth century, when Foxdale and Laxey came into the first rank as producers. As an indication of the prosperity of the Laxey Mining Company, its £80 shares were selling at £1,000 to £1,100 in 1852, while they reached £1,200 in 1854. In the latter year was erected the famous Laxey Wheel (which was said to be the largest in the world) for pumping water out of the mines. Mining reached its heyday during the seventies and eighties of last century when the production figures for lead, silver, and zinc reached their highest limits.

In 1876 the value of the ore shipped from Laxey alone was £90,915, while the value of the products of the Foxdale mines was never less than £40,000 during the period between 1858 and 1864. Taking the total output of Manx mines together, the figure for lead-ore in 1885 was 6,868 tons, while in 1878, 11,898 tons of zinc-ore were produced, and in 1877, 186,019 ozs. of silver. Even in regard to iron-ore, the Manx mines produced 2,256 tons in 1873, and in 1865 they produced 1,317 tons of copper. Precise figures of the number of people employed are not available, but in 1848 it was estimated there were 300 at Laxey and 350 at Foxdale. Later on the numbers increased, and it may be estimated that, during the period between 1855 and 1880, the mining industry in the Island as a whole absorbed well over 1,000 men. Since then there has been a steady decline owing to the competition from the workings at Broken Hill and elsewhere, so that now even the richest mines—Laxey and Foxdale—have closed down. The decay of the mines caused an extensive emigration of Manx miners to the gold-fields of South Africa and Australia, as well as to various parts of the United States, where their descendants may now be found in appreciable numbers (Fig. 46).

The Visiting or Tourist Industry

The Island possesses a capital asset of very great value in the magnificent scenery of her mountains, glens and coasts so that, in modern times, catering for summer visitors has come to be the most important of Manx industries, and the one on which most of the other activities of the Island depend, directly or indirectly. As in the case of most of the other British tourist centres the main development came during the later part of the nineteenth century, so that whereas about 20,000 to 30,000 visitors came every year between 1830 and 1840, by 1873, when the Victoria Pier was opened at Douglas, the number had increased to 90,000. That number was doubled during the next ten years, and thus in 1884 over 187,000 arrived. Progress continued rapidly, and by 1901 the figure had risen to over 418,000. The highest recorded figure before the second World War was in 1913 when there was a total of 615,726; and the nearest approach to that was in 1937 when 583,037 visitors arrived. Since 1945 the number of tourists has again been mounting rapidly, and in 1947 a new high peak was reached with a total of 618,847, of whom 25,578 travelled by air.

The great majority of these tourists were from England, and in 1929 (the last year for which such details were published), over 86 per cent of the total came from Liverpool, Fleetwood, Heysham and some smaller north-western ports. Liverpool with 50 per cent and Fleetwood with 30 per cent were clearly of primary importance. The contribution from the Scottish ports was only just over 6 per cent of the total, while that from Ireland amounted to 5.5 per cent (3.3 per cent from Dublin and the remainder from the Ulster ports).

During the peak period of the season in early August, the vast numbers of people who have to be transported by boat present some unique problems. As many as 68,372 passengers have been embarked and disembarked at Douglas in one day, (Aug. 7th, 1937), and in order to transport them about fifty steamer sailings had to be arranged. There is no traffic quite like this at any cross-Channel port in the British Isles. To provide for this huge annual influx, which has brought wealth hitherto undreamed of, all kinds of improvements have been necessary, such as the harbour works and promenades at Douglas, Ramsey, Peel, Port Erin, and elsewhere. The interior has also been opened up by railways and by a network of roads including the course of one of the world's most famous motor-cycling races, from Douglas via Ballacraine and Glen Helen to Ramsey, and thence back again over the well-known mountain road.

Population Changes

The first official census took place in 1821 when the total population was 40,081. Judging by the calculations that had been made by the clergy during the eighteenth century, this represented a big increase on the previous population of the Island, since according to an estimate made in 1727 the total number of people was then only about 14,400, while it has been suggested by Moore that during the seventeenth century the figure was probably about 12,000. Not only was the population so low in those days but the conditions in which the people lived were very primitive. Sanitation was bad, various diseases such as small-pox and cholera were rampant, and the death-rate must have been very high.

The population apparently rose fairly sharply during the later eighteenth and early nineteenth centuries to reach the figure already given for 1821. After that there was a definite increase each census (except between 1871 and 1881) until 1891, when the normal population reached its maximum of 55,608. Since then the movement has been steadily downward, and the last official census in 1931 returned the total of 49,308*.

In addition to the changes that have occurred in the total population, there has been a profound alteration in the distribution as between the town and the country. In 1726, the total population of the four towns was only 2,530, representing about 17 per cent of the whole Island. Douglas had become slightly the most populous with 810, Castletown having 785, while Peel had 475, and Ramsey 460. By 1821 the town population had reached 11,500 or 28 per cent of the total; but although the country population (28,581) was then relatively less than previously, it was actually twice as much as the total for the whole Island a century before that. Since 1921 there has been a steady movement away from the country districts so that in 1931 the population of the four towns represented 56 per cent of the total. If the village populations in Onchan, Laxey, Port St. Mary, Port Erin and Michael be added to those for the large towns, then the total town population is as high as 67 per cent for the whole Island. Douglas with a total of

*In 1921 the population was returned as 60,284, this being the highest figure ever recorded. There is no doubt, however, that this figure is misleading since it included 11,014 visitors, the census having been taken on June 19-20.

19,329 has far outstripped the others, being followed by Ramsey with 4,198, Peel with 2,477, and Castletown with 1,713.

Despite the increase in population during the later eighteenth and nineteenth centuries, there was always a certain amount of emigration from the Island, the numbers fluctuating according to the degree of prosperity of farming, fishing, and mining. Bad conditions in agriculture meant a considerable emigration to America especially between 1825 and 1837. There was again great distress following the failure of the potato crop in 1846, and large numbers of Manxmen went during the next four or five years to California or to Australia, being attracted by the gold discoveries there. Emigration from the Island continued although not in such large numbers except when mining conditions became very poor; and so it has come about that there are now many thousands of Manx people and their descendants scattered not only throughout Britain but also in North America, South Africa, Australia and New Zealand, while many are to be found serving at the present day, as in the past, in the Royal Navy and the Merchant Navy.

REFERENCES

QUAYLE, THOMAS, *Agriculture in the Isle of Man,* London, 1812.

MEGAW, B. R. S., Corn Growing in Man 4,000 years ago, *Journal of the Manx Museum*, IV, (1939), 119-121.

Workington Agricultural Society's *Reports on Manx Agriculture* for 1807 and 1808.

Report of Committee appointed by Tynwald on Agriculture, Dec. 18th, 1926.

MOORE, A. W., *History*, II, 926-971.

SMITH, W. C., *A Short History of the Irish Sea Herring Fisheries*, 1923; also The Manx Herring Shoals, *Trans. Liverpool Biol. Soc.* LI, 1938.

Manx Herring Fishery Report, (issued annually).

MEGAW, E. M., Manx Fishing Craft, *Journal of the Manx Museum*, V, (1941), 14-16; also, *The Mariner's Mirror*, XXVII (1941).

MOORE, A. W., *Manx Worthies*, Douglas, 1901.

Special Reports on the Mineral Resources of Great Britain (Mem. Geol. Survey), Lead and Zinc Ores (Vol. XXVI, 1923), Copper Ores (Vol. XXX, 1925), contain sections on the Isle of Man.

LAMPLUGH, G. W., *Geology of the Isle of Man*, London, 1903.

Chapter XV.

MODERN TIMES

The year 1866 was a crucial turning point in Manx history and may well be regarded as the one that ushered in the modern phase of the nation's development, both politically and economically. Not only did Man then regain to some extent the right to spend its own money but the people gained the power of choosing their representatives in the House of Keys. At about the same time the Island set out upon a new economic path and resolved to draw a large part of its livelihood from the business of providing food, lodging and recreation for summer visitors. The period that has elapsed since that date has witnessed profound changes in government, business, education, and in the standard of living that have given this phase of the national evolution a particular fascination and significance. The outstanding features of such changes will now be reviewed in outline.

The Government

At present the Government of Man consists of (1) the Lieutenant-Governor who represents the Crown, (2) the Legislative Council, or as it is occasionally termed, the upper house, consisting of ten members (apart from the Governor), (3) the House of Keys, which is the elected chamber, and (4) Tynwald, or as it is sometimes, but less correctly, referred to as the Tynwald Court, which consists of the Governor and the two branches of the legislature sitting together.

If the Isle of Man had had the kind of constitution which exists in Great Britain, the Governor would have been advised and assisted by a 'cabinet' of ministers whose duty it would have been to recommend to him and to Tynwald what laws should be passed, and to take charge of the various departments of government as they are carried on day by day. But in 1866, cabinet government was not considered suitable for a community of this size, and the Lieutenant-Governor, who is appointed by the King, remained supreme head of the Government; and part of his duty has been to make sure that the Island does not get into debt by spending more than it has received. He is thus his own Chancellor of the Exchequer with financial responsibility and a complete veto on any financial proposals that Tynwald might make. He is also his own Home Secretary, and the police are directly under his control. He presides over the Legislative Council and also over Tynwald, but he is not in charge of such departments as are entrusted to boards (e.g. the Highway and Transport Board, and Board of Education) although he has power to limit the amount of money these boards can spend. Hence over a vast range of subjects his authority is very considerable, and it is clear that the government of the Island depends for much of its smooth and harmonious working, or otherwise, on the experience and the judgment of the Governor.

Up to the time of Lord Raglan, who was appointed in 1902 and who left the Island in 1919, no time limit had been imposed on the appointment of governors. Since then the period of office has been definitely fixed, the limit now being seven years. This has not been exceeded except in one instance, that of Earl Granville, whose seven years of office expired during World War II, and who for special reasons was asked to remain for an additional year.

The Legislative Council

The consent of the Legislative Council as well as the consent of the Keys is necessary before any law can be passed. Although the functions of the Council and of the British House of Lords are now very much the same in this respect, the history and composition of these two institutions are very different. The Legislative Council has developed from a body called 'the lord's council' which existed in the fifteenth century when it consisted of the lord's officers, those who collected the revenues and helped the Governor (in former times styled the 'Lieutenant' or the 'Captain') to manage the lord's business and keep his records. In the course of time there have been added to this body the principal officers of the law, the Deemsters and the lord's attorney (now termed the Attorney-General), and the principal officers of the church, the Bishop, Archdeacon and Vicar General—the official who advises the bishop on points of law. Until quite recent days the Council met in private and discussed any proposed legislation with the

Governor, advising him whether or not it was appropriate.

Prior to 1919 the Manx upper house was composed entirely of officials; it contained no representatives of the people, and five of its members were appointed by the British Government. The remaining three represented the religious aspect in the life of the nation, but they had obtained their places in the legislature at a time when there was only one organised religious group in the Island.

An agitation was begun for constitutional reform during the later nineteenth century, and in 1911 the British Government had Manx problems investigated by a special committee presided over by Lord MacDonnell. Most of this committee's recommendations were carried into effect by the Isle of Man Constitution Amendment Act, 1919—the delay that had occurred in carrying out the proposals having been due, partially at any rate, to the intervention of the first World War. The officials who remained as members of the Council after its reform were the Bishop, the Attorney-General and the two Deemsters, while those who were removed comprised the Archdeacon, the Vicar General and the Receiver General.* An entirely new element was introduced into the Council by the addition of four members elected by the Keys and two appointed by the Governor. Each of these elected and appointed members sits for eight years, but the eight-year period does not begin for them all at the same time; half of them retire, and are eligible for re-election or re-appointment every fourth year.

Besides the two Deemsters there had been a senior judge styled the Clerk of the Rolls. The latter office became vacant by death in 1918 and was never filled up, but since then the First Deemster has performed the special duties which belonged to the other office, and the phrase ' Clerk of the Rolls ' has been added to his title. While the judges numbered three, two of them were always available for the hearing of appeals against a judgment given by a third. When the clerkship of the rolls was amalgamated with that of the First Deemster it was provided

*While the Receiver General thus ceased to be *ex-officio* a member of the Legislative Council, a member of the Council was appointed Chairman of the Harbour Board and so became Receiver General. But following the legislation passed in 1949 this title has now ceased to be used.

that some British barrister of eminence should be appointed to sit in the Manx Court of Appeal.

The Keys

The character of the House of Keys which was reformed in 1866 has been sufficiently discussed in Chapter XIII, and no further description is necessary except to note that all of its members, as well as the elected and appointed members of the Council, now receive a payment of £150 a year to cover travelling and other out-of-pocket expenses.

Tynwald (Fig. 48)

This body has no parallel in the other parts of the British Isles since it consists of the Keys and the Legislative Council sitting together, and, as already seen, the Governor presides over Tynwald. All bills passed in the branches must be signed in Tynwald before they are submitted for the royal assent. Tynwald is not a legislative body and could not alter any bill; but the signature to a bill must be given by the Governor and two of the members of the Council then present and by thirteen of the Keys.*

The principal functions of Tynwald are to levy the taxes, and, subject to the Governor's right of veto and the approval of the British Treasury, to decide how the national revenue shall be spent; and to appoint committees, or Boards as many of them are called, to administer defined departments of government.

Boards of Tynwald

These committees of Tynwald represent another distinctive feature of the Manx political system. They perform duties which in Great Britain are performed by ministers chosen by the Prime Minister, and holding office so long as the House of Commons approves the policy of the cabinet as a whole. At the present time, Boards of Tynwald, appointed from its members, and in some cases assisted by representatives of local authorities and of cultural organisations, and financed wholly or partly by votes from the Insular revenue, administer

*It should be noted, however, that the Deemsters continue to sign bills separately in accordance with long established custom.

education, highways, harbours, airports, health and the various social services, fishing, agriculture, advertising, forestry, town and country planning, and the Manx Museum. The total sum annually expended by these Boards in their respective public services amounts to over £860,000. In recent years other Boards have been set up to administer the supply of electricity outside the Douglas area and to provide water supplies over the whole of the Island. As will be seen later, the chairmen of all these Boards are appointed by Tynwald on the recommendation of the Governor.

The Speaker

Since the Keys not only meet in their own chamber but sit with the Council in Tynwald, there is a considerable difference in function between the Speaker of the House of Keys and the Speaker of the House of Commons. It is sometimes remarked upon as curious that the holder of the latter office is called the Speaker although he does not speak but confines himself to the duties of Chairman. But if the rights and privileges of the House are challenged, the Speaker must defend them; and if something has to be said in the name of the whole House he has the responsibility of saying it. The word speaker really means 'spokesman,' one who speaks on behalf of others, and it may be remarked that in the days of arbitrary kingship the Speaker 'spoke for' the House against the King, as, for example, in the case of Speaker Lenthall and Charles I. The Speaker of the Keys occupies this position, particularly when facing the Council and facing the Governor. Since he is not chairman of Tynwald, he may speak on ordinary subjects as a private member. But on occasions of crisis there is no leader of the House such as there would be under a ministry, and the Speaker himself must act as leader. The character and personality of the Speaker must, therefore, count for a great deal in guiding the Island's political life.

Local Government

Popular control has also been extended in this direction. By the Towns Act, 1852, commissioners had been appointed for the four towns of the Island, primarily to look after questions of sanitation. In 1886 the Local Government Act was passed, and under this measure, together with various acts amending it, commissioners have been formed for every parish and for several village districts, to whom increasing powers have been given from time to time. The development of the towns and villages has been largely the work of the commissioners, who have established sewerage works, provided water, maintained roads, dealt with infectious disease, cleared slums, established fever hospitals, abattoirs, public baths, libraries and recreation grounds, and in some areas have provided workmen's houses. They have also controlled the erection of new buildings and generally provided the amenities of modern life. In 1896, Douglas was created a municipal borough with a mayor, six alderman and eighteen councillors.

Education

The period since 1886 has witnessed remarkable progress in the educational sphere. As a result of the great Manx Education Act of 1872, which laid the basis for the development of sound education for all, school boards were formed in every town and parish district, and free elementary education came into force in 1892. In one important respect the Manx Act differed from the English Act of 1870. Bible instruction was compulsory in every provided school, with the result that when all the old parochial schools carried on by the church were handed over to the new school boards, this change was achieved with little disturbance of the religious atmosphere. In 1894 the first higher grade school was established, and this has ultimately led to the formation of the secondary schools for boys and girls at Douglas, Ramsey and Castletown.

Despite what might seem to have been such promising beginnings, the position that had developed by 1911 had some very unsatisfactory features which were condemned in no uncertain manner in the report of the MacDonnell Committee to which reference has already been made. In the sphere of elementary education there were twenty-one separate school areas in the Island, and there were four higher education authorities, one in each High Bailiff's district. The result was that the management was excessively parochial while the quality of the education and the housing and equipment left much to be desired. A more unified system was strongly advocated; and

Fig. 48.—Tynwald in session. The members of the Legislative Council are on the elevated bench with the Governor presiding. Below the latter is the Speaker with the Keys on either side of the hall.

Fig. 49.—King and Queen at St. John's (Tynwald) 1945

the Island was urged to provide more funds for education in general, as well as greater facilities for higher education.

Since then very substantial progress has been made. There is now one elected Education Authority which administers secondary and elementary education in the Island as a whole under the general supervision of the Board of Education, which is appointed by Tynwald; and a number of modern buildings have been erected, e.g. at Rushen, Laxey and Pulrose, although many of the older buildings still survive. Additional secondary education accommodation has been provided by the erection of the Ramsey Grammar School and the Castle Rushen Secondary School in addition to the separate High Schools for Boys and Girls in Douglas. In the years preceding the second World War the number of pupils attending the secondary schools in the Island (including King William's College and the Buchan School for Girls in Castletown) per head of the population, was definitely higher in Man than in either England or Wales.*

The Education Act of 1948 brought the Manx educational system into complete line with the system established in England by the 'Butler' Act of 1944; and the Island is operating the multilateral system of higher education for all children aged more than eleven by giving all of them teaching of a similar character for the first two years, and then allowing their education to divide into different 'streams,' the academic and the practical, according to their varying aptitudes. The Island has been fortunate in possessing suitable buildings which have made this possible.

Some Aspects of the Manx Financial System

When the British Government restored to Tynwald the general right to spend the proceeds of Manx taxation it refused to surrender its control completely. The Isle of Man Customs and Harbours Act, passed by Parliament in 1866, transferred the Manx customs revenue from the British Exchequer to the Island's revenue, but stipulated that certain fundamental costs

*In 1935 the number of pupils per 1,000 of the population was 20.1 in the Isle of Man, as compared with 11.3 in England and Wales (England alone — 10.8; Wales alone — 17.9). As a measure of the increased financial support given to education in recent years it may be noted that, whereas in 1910 the expenditure out of public revenue on education services was about £16,000, in 1948 it was over £200,000.

of government, such as the expenses of the law courts and the police, and the salaries of the Governor and of the staff of Government Office, were to be deducted before any part of the customs revenue was placed at Tynwald's disposal. This class of expenditure is described in Budgets from 1914 onwards under the heading of the 'reserved services,' and, not withstanding the protestations of the Keys, it has been retained in the hands of the British Government. The remaining kinds of expenditure, called the 'voted services,' have been sanctioned by Tynwald, but the resolutions of this body are liable to be vetoed by the Governor, and in any case they do not become effective until approved by the British Treasury as laid down in the Act of 1866, amended by an Act passed in 1887. It is, indeed, the case that a strict interpretation of these Acts would mean that Tynwald would have no power to spend a penny of the Island's revenue until a surplus had been ascertained at the end of the year, and then the money could only be expended out of the accumulated fund during the succeeding year. In practice the system has developed whereby the Governor prepares a Budget in anticipation of the year's income and expenditure, when the income estimated in a way which satisfies the Treasury may be voted and spent during the year in which it is earned.

Traditionally, most of the Manx revenue is derived from customs and excise duties, and even at the present day two thirds of the total amount is obtained in this way. A fundamental feature in connection with this taxation is that the duties are, with a few exceptions,* kept identical with those of Great Britain, thus facilitating the collection of the customs and also removing the possibility of a revival of the old smuggling 'mischief.' This task is performed by the United Kingdom customs authorities and paid for by the Island on an agreed percentage.

With the continual increase of the duties and the development of the tourist industry during the later part of the nineteenth century, it became increasingly necessary to simplify the procedure of collecting the Manx customs; and in 1894 negotiations between the Insular authorities and the British

*The chief exception is beer on which the duties are lower in the Island, and in this case the duties are levied in the Island.

Treasury resulted in an arrangement known as the 'common purse,' which has regulated the whole matter ever since.

The Common Purse Scheme

Under this arrangement the duties on goods which are consigned to Man are collected by the British customs authorities, so that it is necessary to determine what proportion represents the Island's share. This is based on what is called the 'fiscal population' of Man, and to obtain this for any year there must be added to the resident population, as recorded in the census returns, some figure representing the visitors to the Island. Such a fiscal equivalent for visitors is arrived at on the results of decennial tests in which the actual imports of various commodities are ascertained under the provisions of the Revenue Returns Acts of 1894 and 1895. In this way the total Insular fiscal population can be calculated for each year, and the share of the total customs receipts due to the Isle of Man can be ascertained. Thus for the year 1929, when the actual visiting population was 599,048, the fiscal equivalent was equal to 38,156, which, when added to the resident population of 49,078, gave a total fiscal population of 87,234. The Insular Government thus received for that year a share of any duty imposed in common represented by the proportion which 87,234 bore to the total population of the United Kingdom. If the Manx duty on any article is higher or lower than the British duty, or is not imposed for the same period, that article falls out of the common purse, and duty would be collected on its removal into the Island through the customs.

Up to the war of 1914-18 the Manx revenue continued to be derived entirely from indirect taxation, almost all in the form of customs and excise duties; but in 1918 income tax was imposed for the first time, though the rate was much lower than that which prevailed in Great Britain in that year, and it has continued to be lower.

Financial and Political Relations with the British Government

It is vitally important that the relationships between the Manx and British Governments should be friendly and harmonious. If the British Government exercised its powers autocratically the Island would have very little opportunity to manage its own affairs in the way that the Manx nation passionately desires to do. On the part of the Isle of Man, the occasional interference by the Home Office and the Treasury, and the very fact that these departments have the power to interfere, have caused much resentment. Contrariwise, there has been at any rate one period when the British Government thought the attitude taken up on behalf of the Isle of Man deserved some candid criticism. The Manx Government, it was considered, possessed a large amount of money and could fairly easily place itself in possession of more, and yet it was not making an adequate contribution towards the cost of the first World War.

After 1918, it was a fact that the Island's income had increased four-fold as compared with pre-war years. Whereas before 1914 the total revenue had been about £85,000, in 1921 it was £369,000 while there was, in addition, an accumulated fund in the latter year of £338,000. It may be observed that income-tax in 1921 produced less than one-tenth of the total revenue, the remainder being largely from customs duties which had undergone such a marked increase during the war years. Despite this enhanced revenue, the annual contribution to the British Exchequer, then grappling with the huge war debt, was only £10,000 as it had been fixed in 1866. Obviously there was a strong case for some increase in the Manx contribution but the problem was to fix an equitable sum, having regard to all the factors concerned.

Tynwald in 1921 assumed liability for British War Stock to the value of £250,000 to be paid off in twenty years. This meant that an additional payment of £20,000 a year would be made to the British Government over and above the statutory £10,000 already provided for. This amount was thought to be inadequate by the British authorities, and a Committee of the Privy Council was appointed in 1923 to consider the matter. The Committee decided to advise the British Government to demand £100,000 a year for fifty years, and £50,000 a year thereafter in place of the £10,000 annual contribution fixed in 1866. These proposals raised a storm of protest in the Island, since, not only was the amount considered quite excessive, but the whole principle of the Island's control of its finances was attacked.

A satisfactory settlement of the problem was reached in 1926 when the Tynwald decided to take over another half million of British war debt, and in 1932-33 the balance of the debt then outstanding was actually liquidated by way of a local loan. On the political side, a result of equal, if not greater, significance was the fact that, not only did the Island assert its right to decide the amount of the contribution to be made to Britain, but also in the words of the Governor, Sir Claude Hill, ' an atmosphere of mutual trust ' was created between the Manx and British Governments which was of vital importance in solving any further problems between the two countries. As an indication of the greater feeling of harmony that developed, it may be observed that, in 1938, Tynwald, without any suggestion or request from the British Government voted a sum of £100,000 towards the cost of re-armament which Parliament was then facing, and since that has made further contributions to the cost of the second World War amounting in all to £1,750,000, with an additional £500,000 on loan free of interest.

Conditions since the Second World War

Despite the gifts which have just been indicated it is widely felt at the present day that conditions have been altered so radically since 1939 that the financial arrangements between the Island and the United Kingdom should be reviewed and placed upon a footing more in accord with existing circumstances. There is, for example, now a much larger income derived from customs duties than before the war owing to the substantial increases imposed by the United Kingdom to assist in raising the vast sums of money required for defence and other matters; and as an indication of the substantial benefits thus accruing to the Island it may be observed that whereas the common purse allocation was £287,600 in 1925-26 it was estimated at £1,600,000 for the year 1948-49. Yet the fixed annual contribution which the Isle of Man makes towards the cost of Imperial defence and other common services still remains at £10,000 which was originally decided upon in 1866.

With a view to finding a satisfactory basis for a new permanent arrangement which would include an increased contribution in relation to the Island's ability to pay, negotiations have been taking place between the Manx authorities and the Home Office, and a unanimous decision on the matter was reached at a meeting of Tynwald on November 15th, 1949. In accordance with this, an Isle of Man Act is to be passed authorising the Manx Government to pay to the British Exchequer a sum equal to 5 per cent of the common purse receipts for the year in which the payment is to be made, such sum to include the amount of £10,000 a year at present paid under the Act of 1866. It is proposed that this arrangement will begin on April 1st, 1950, and will last in the first instance for five years, while provision will also be made for Tynwald, with the consent of the Governor after consultation with the branches, to increase or decrease the sum referred to. Based on the estimated receipts from duties falling into the common purse arrangements for the year ending March 31st, 1950, the amount of the Manx contribution would be £80,000. Finally, it may be noted that a fresh Act of Parliament will be necessary to repeal the Act of 1866, and to make provision for the allocation of the revenue from customs duties between the governments of the United Kingdom and the Isle of Man.

This subject of an increased contribution arose when Tynwald was following up an aspect of greater financial control which had been left over after the political reforms of 1946, which will be described on a later page. It had then been proposed that financial administration should be 'simplified' in various ways, but principally by the Governor being authorised to signify Treasury approval promptly, except when he felt that it was a matter of special importance which ought to be discussed with the British Government. This offer was now confirmed in such a way that it would apply to the 'reserved services' as well as the 'voted services' so that Tynwald's freedom of action would be greatly enlarged.

Manx Taxation

As regards taxation there is no doubt that a certain disparity exists as between the Island and Great Britain; and criticism has been levelled from time to time at the relative lowness of the Manx rates. In 1911 it was estimated that taxation per head in Great Britain was £3 6s. 0d., whereas in Man it was only about £1 7s. 0d. This difference arose from the fact that the Manx were exempt from most forms of direct taxation including income tax, stamps, death and estate duties. As regards indirect taxation it has already been seen that very little difference exists in the matter of customs duties.

At the present day the position is still the same as far as indirect taxation is concerned, but a direct tax exists in the form of income tax, the rate of which has been gradually increased since it was introduced in 1918. It is, nevertheless, difficult to make any precise comparison between the relative taxation per head in Man and Great Britain since income tax in the former is levied by means of a graduated scale, the rates for the year 1948-49 varying from 2/- to 3/6d. in the pound. In future it is proposed to have a new standard rate of 4/- in the pound. Since 1940 surtax has been levied at varying rates on incomes in excess of £2,000.

The Manx case for the justification of the lower rate of taxation is based on the relative isolation of the Island as well as its poverty in natural resources and supplies of capital, combined with the particular circumstances affecting the tourist industry, on whose prosperity now depends the whole economic structure of Man. It is urged that in order to reach the Island a very appreciable additional sum must be spent on steamer fares by the holidaymakers, most of whom come from the densely peopled industrial areas of northern England. To offset the greater costs of travel, some relief from the English rate of taxation must be afforded to the businesses providing entertainments and accommodation so that they may be able to offer cheaper amusements and, to some extent, cheaper food and drink as a tourist attraction. Secondly, since people taking up residence in the Isle of Man are not so easily able to visit or receive visits from relatives or friends, or to enjoy the famous picture galleries and the great concerts and plays, some inducement is felt to be necessary to encourage the relatively small number of older people with modest incomes from all over the British Commonwealth and Empire who choose to live in the Island on their retirement.

In the absence from the Island of the kinds of manufacturing industries that are found in England and also in Northern Ireland, it is certain that the taxable capacity of Man cannot be compared with that of the other two countries. As an illustration of this it has been estimated that to produce a comparable yield of income and surtax with England on a population basis, the Isle of Man would have to impose an income tax of 12/- in the pound, and a correspondingly increased surtax. On the other hand, as already seen, any steep increase in income tax would not only react very unfavourably on the amusement and transport companies, and on the visiting industry generally, but it would also tend to drive away the residential population since they would lose one of the advantages which counter-balance the many disadvantages of living on the Island.

Modern Political Developments— The Consultative Committee of the Keys

In 1921, after a dispute with the Governor over an increase in official salaries, the Keys obtained from the Home Secretary an increase in their rights over finance. It was provided that before additions were made in the 'reserved services,' the Governor should ask the opinions of each of the branches. He was not obliged to accept these opinions, but the possibility was ended of salaries being increased without Tynwald's knowledge. Before the Budget was prepared for any one year, the Governor was to lay before each branch a statement of proposed taxation and expenditure, and to give them time for making their comments or their counter-proposals. There was no further possibility, either, of Tynwald being pressed to pass a Budget on not more than two or three day's notice.

To make these preliminary Budget discussions more effective, the Home Secretary suggested that the Keys should set up a Finance Committee, which would examine the Governor's proposals before they were submitted to the full House. The Keys appointed their committee accordingly; but in recent years it has in practice been amalgamated with another body called the Keys Consultative Committee, which the Governor, Sir Claude Hill, asked the Keys to appoint in 1927 as a committee which he could consult, when desired, upon legislation and administration. Sir Claude Hill had these consultations from time to time, but his successor, Sir Montagu Butler, developed the practice by calling in the Consultative Committee much more regularly. This system enables the Governor to learn the views of the Keys, and the Keys to learn the views of the Governor, before legislation is proposed or any administrative policy put into action.

The Executive Council of Tynwald (1946)

During the second World War consultation between the Governor and a selected body representing Tynwald was greatly enlarged by the setting up of an Advisory Committee. The Governor adopted the practice of having a weekly meeting with this body, and he found it so useful that he brought before it matters relating to the general government of the Island as well as those specifically related to the war. In this way the Governor not only had the benefit of the Committee's advice but he was also assured of substantial support when matters came up for discussion before Tynwald. After the war it was felt that a more permanent body somewhat in the nature of a ' cabinet ' should be instituted to replace the wartime committee; and the initiative in the discussions that followed between Tynwald and the Home Office was taken by the Speaker of the House of Keys, Mr. J. D. Qualtrough.

The outcome of these discussions was that the Home Secretary, in February 1946, expressed full sympathy with the proposal that the Governor should be assisted by an Executive Council composed of seven members of Tynwald, the majority being persons who have been elected by Tynwald as chairmen of five principal spending Boards, and the remainder being recommended by Tynwald but not necessarily chairmen of Boards. The creation of this Executive Council is regarded as one of the greatest constitutional developments the Island has ever known and its future will be followed with great interest. It was actually constituted in October 1946; and at its meetings, normally weekly, the Governor presides, while the Government Secretary and the Attorney General are in attendance. All matters affecting the Government of the Island are considered by the Council which advises the Governor thereon, and in practice the Governor accepts the advice of the Executive.

In conformity with the developments which have just been indicated, the various Boards of Tynwald have been reorganised and reconstituted; and now the five chief ones are those dealing with:—(*a*) Local Government, (*b*) Agriculture and Fisheries, (*c*) Highway and Transport, (*d*) Social Services, and (*e*) Education. Formerly the chairman of each Board was elected by its own members but now he is elected by Tynwald on the recommendation of the Governor after consultation with representative members of that body.

Economic, Social and Cultural Progress

On the economic side, the Island has come to rely more and more definitely on the tourist industry as the predominant source of its livelihood. No doubt, in 1866, it was thought that there would in future be several forms of employment; indeed at that time much money was being made in mining, and although fishing was subject to chance and change, it was destined for many years afterwards to be very prosperous. But now the first of these older industries has died out while the other has shrunk to a very low ebb; and agriculture, which certainly could not support itself by export trade, is very closely linked with its local and seasonal market—a market clearly of high value. One result of the changed conditions is that, in normal years, about one thousand men in the Island who find employment during three months or so in the summer, cannot obtain ordinary work during the rest of the year, and they are provided with work such as road construction, afforestation, and land drainage, by the national government and by the governing bodies of the towns. The employment of available labour in this way has been considered costly but it has probably proved abundantly worth while. The result has not only enabled the Island to keep its place as a first-class visiting resort, but has contributed in no small measure to public health, as well as to the pleasure and prosperity of its people. If the Island had not developed as a holiday resort, a much larger proportion of its population might have been forced to leave it; and, on the contrary, in recent years, a good many people have come into it in order to carry on the business of catering for holiday-makers, so that the population of the Island is tending to become more mixed.

As a result of the large earnings brought into the Island by the tourist industry, and through the influence of the holidaymakers, as well as the greater contact with other people, the Manx have learnt new standards of living, as witness the striking social and educational developments that have already been traced; and conditions are now profoundly different from what they were in our parents' or grandparents' days. Against these benefits, it is felt by some that the Island has suffered by the great flood of English and other influences which overwhelmed the Manx language until it threatened to become quite extinct, while other treasured Manx characteristics seem in danger of being swept away.

As the high tide of the visiting traffic recedes at the end of every summer, the rest of the year is spent more in accordance with the Manx people's own inclinations. A definite revival of the Manx national spirit has been showing itself notably in such organisations as *Yn Cheshaght Ghailckagh* (the Manx Society), *Aeglagh Vannin* (the Young Manx) and the World Manx Association. In connection with the quickening of interest in Manx history and culture, perhaps one of the most significant events of modern times has been the establishment of the Manx Museum, Library and Art Gallery opened in 1922, which has rapidly become the great treasure house of the Island's story. The work of the Museum has been extended during recent years, and with remarkable success, by the initiation of an open-air museum in Cregneash (the first of its kind in the British Isles), and by the opening of a folk-culture gallery with a specimen farm-house in the Museum itself. Moreover, several classes exist for the study of the Manx language so as to save it from extinction, although it must, of course, be realised that under the conditions of the modern world the possession of a separate language is, in itself, no longer regarded as the predominant feature of a distinctive nationality. General culture is promoted by the intensely popular Manx Music Festival (founded in 1892), held in the spring, which was recently enlarged by the inclusion of competitions in drama (with a special section for plays in the Manx dialect), and which for many years included competitions in the arts and crafts.

Side by side with these developments have been the struggles, which have already been traced, to secure that degree of financial and political independence which would not only preserve the ancient constitution but also give the Island adequate control over its own affairs, and at the same time enable its people to contribute their due share towards the cost of maintaining those privileges which they enjoy as an integral part of the British Isles. Thus would the twin objectives of independence and inter-dependence be brought into harmony. In the wider sphere, the recognition of the position of Man as a distinct and separate entity within the British Commonwealth of peoples is being more and more assured, and an interesting reflection of this is the recent enrolment of the Manx Legislature among the members of the British Empire Parliamentary Association of Dominions and Colonies.

During the second World War the Island had a proud record of service in the contributions made by its men and women in the various branches of the armed forces, while, in addition, a considerable number of men served in the Merchant Navy. Reference may also be made to the services rendered by the Manx boats in the Dunkirk evacuation, during which some of the latest and best ships of the fleet of steamers were lost, while others were lost in the North African campaign. Three of the Manx vessels ferried many thousands of soldiers in the invasion of Normandy. Moreover, the Island, in common with every part of the United Kingdom, was utilised for various purposes connected with the defence of the realm, and the numerous facilities offered by the strategic position of the Isle of Man were fully appreciated by the British Government and were extensively used. Here may be mentioned the erection of the radar research stations, and the construction or enlarging of the aerodromes at Jurby and Ronaldsway; and the further development of aviation seems destined to play a very significant role in the future history of the Island as the sea has done in the past.

REFERENCES

Report of the Departmental Committee on the Constitution, etc., of the Isle of Man, (Chairman, Lord MacDonnell), H.M. Stationery Office, 1911. Vol. II, consisting of Minutes of Evidence and Appendices, was published in 1912.

SARGEAUNT, B. E., *An Outline of the Financial System of the Isle of Man Government*, Douglas, 1925.

Report of the Committee of the Privy Council on the question of contributions to the Imperial funds from the Isle of Man, Jersey, etc., Parl. Papers, Session 1926, VIII, 367-450.
NORRIS, S., *Manx Memories and Movements*, Douglas, 1938.
Estimates of Receipts and Expenditure, published annually, Douglas.
Supplement to the Isle of Man Government Gazette, No. 101, (1944). This contains a Memorandum by the Legislative Council on the Keys' proposals for constitutional reform, and also a Minute of a joint meeting of members of the Legislative Council and the House of Keys held on the floor of the Tynwald Chamber, on 25th April, 1944.
How the Isle of Man is Governed: A Study in Constitutional Law and Practice. (Reprinted from the Isle of Man Weekly Times), Douglas, 1944.

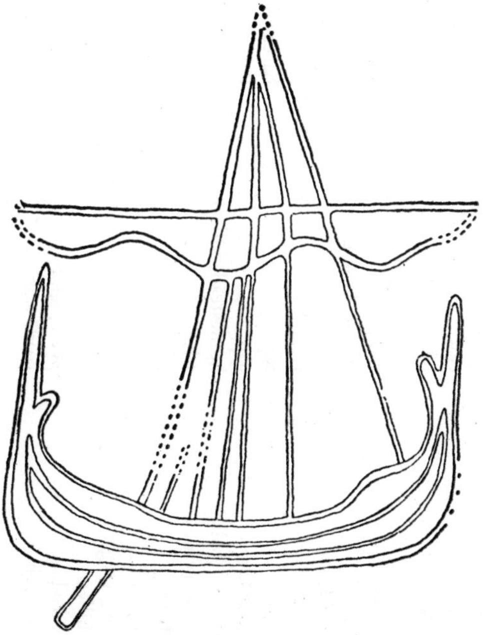

Fig. 50.—Viking Ship, Hedin Cross, Maughold.

GLOSSARY OF WORDS MOST OFTEN FOUND IN MANX PLACE-NAMES

A.	*Manx Gaelic*	*English*	*Examples*
1	aah	ford	Ballanea (Mx. *Balley 'n aah*) = farm of the ford.
2	aittin	gorse	Cronk Aittin = gorse hill.
3	ar, hiar	east	Garee har = east shrubbery; Cashtal Ar = east castle.
4	arbyl	tail	Niarbyl (Mx. *Yn Arbyl*) = the tail.
5	ard	high, height	Cashtal yn ard = castle of the height.
6	arragh	rampart	Kione Arragh = end of the rampart.
7	arrey	watch, look-out	Cronk ny Arrey Laa = hill of the day watch.
8	aspick	bishop	Garee Aspick = Bishop's shrubbery (Parville).
9	awin	river	Awin Vitchel = Michael's river.
10	baare	top	Bareavolly = top or crest of the old road.
11	baarney	gap	Barnagh = red gap (Mx. *Baarney jiarg*).
12	balley (balla)	homestead, village, town	Ballaquark = Quark's farm; Ballachrink = hill farm
13	bane (vane)	white	Clagh Vane Voalley = white stone wall (name of a cliff at Aldrick).
14	bayr	road	Bayr ny pollagh = road of the pools.
15	beeal	mouth	Bealna (Mx. *Beeal yn aah*) = mouth of the ford.
16	beg (veg)	little	Ballabeg = little farm; Cabbyl veg = little horse (rock).
17	billey	tree	Ballavilley = tree farm.
18	boayl	place, spot	Boayl ny carn = place of the cairns.
19	bollagh	road, track	Bollagh Jiarg = red road (see also No. 10).
20	breck	speckled	Cronk breck = speckled hill; Brecky = speckled place.
21	breid	gorge	Eary breid = shieling of the gorge; Braid Foss = waterfall gorge.
22	breinn	stinking	Poyll Breinn = stinking pool (on shore).
23	brisht	broken	Broogh vrisht = broken bank or brow (road leading from St. John's to Slieau Whuallian).
24	broogh	brink, brow	See No. 23.

25	buigh	yellow	Reeast buigh = yellow moor.
26	bwoaillee	cattle fold	Bollybane (Mx. *Bwoaillee bane*) = white fold.
27	cabbal	chapel	Faaie ny Cabbal = flat or green of the chapel.
28	cabbyl	horse	See No. 16.
29	cam	crooked	Camlork = crooked or winding ridge.
30	carn	tumulus, cairn	See No. 18.
31	carnane	rocky hill, cairn	Carnanes = rocky hills.
32	carrick	large rock	Carrick = large rock (giving its name to Baie ny Carrickey); Carrick y Voddey = the rock of the dog.
33	cashtal	castle, earthwork	See No. 5.
34	cass, cosh	foot	Cass Strooan = stream foot or end (shore at Lhergy Doo).
35	cassan	footpath	Gob ny cassan = point of the path.
36	cheu	side	Cheu yn Phurt = the harbour side (Manx name for North Quay, Douglas).
37	chiarn	lord	Pairk y Chiarn = the Lord's pasture field.
38	chibbyr	well	Chibbyr y Vashtee = well of the baptism.
39	chirrym	dry	Balley Chirrym = dry farm (now Ballacottier).
40	claddagh	river meadow	Claddagh wuigh = yellow river-meadow.
41	clagh	stone	Magher ny Clagh = field of the stone (Bishopscourt).
42	cleigh	fence	Magher cleigh roauyr = field of the thick hedge.
43	coan	hollow	Ballachoan = farm of the hollow.
44	conney	gorse (for firewood)	Conocan = a place of firewood.
45	cooill	corner, nook	The Cooil = the nook.
46	coon	narrow	Glion coon = the narrow glen (within Groudle Glen).
47	cor	small round hill	Close Cordias = close of the south hill.
48	creagh	boundary	Cronk y Cree = hill of the end or boundary.
49	creen	ripe, withered	Crowcreen = withered tree.
50	creg (plur. creggyn)	rock	Creg Inneen Thalleyr = rock of the tailor's daughter.
51	creggan	rocky place	Creggan mooar = great craggy place.

A.	*Manx Gaelic*	*English*	*Examples*
52	cronk (plur. chrink)	hill	Cronk Keeill Eoin = hill of John's church (Manx name of Tynwald Hill). See also No. 12.
53	crosh	cross	Ballacrosha = cross farm.
54	crossag	crossing, bridge	Crossag = crossing (Monk's Bridge).
55	curragh	marsh, mire	Ballacurry = marsh farm; Curragh mollagh = rough marsh.
56	darragh	oak	Cronk Darragh = oak hill
57	dhone	brown	Crot William Done = brown (haired) William's croft.
58	doarlish	gap	Doarlish ny mwaagh = gap of the hares.
59	dhoo	black	Cronk Doo Ling = black hill of the ling.
60	doon	fort	Dhoon (from Mx. *Kerroo Doon*) = fort quarterland.
61	dowin	deep	Dhoon (Mx. Dowin) = deep place (on Arragon Mooar).
62	dreeym	back, ridge	Dreemlang = long ridge.
63	drine	thorn	Driney = thorny place.
64	droghad	bridge	Droughad Fayle = Fayle's bridge.
65	eairkan	lapwing	Close ny eairkan = close of the lapwing.
66	eary	shieling, hill-pasture	Eairystane = Stein's (for Thorstein's) shieling.
67	eas, as	waterfall	Ballanass = farm of the waterfall.
68	eaynin	precipice	Broogh ny eaynin = brow of the precipice (on Glen Roy river).
69	edd	nest	Burrow Nedd = nest hill (See No. 162 for first element which is Norse. and No. 74).
70	eean	bird	Traie ein = bird's shore.
71	eear, heear, sheear	west	Garee heear = west shrubbery (fields on Ballagawne).
72	faaie	a flat or green	Faaie ny cooag = flat of the cuckoo.
73	fannag	crow	Broogh ny fannag = brow or bank of the crow.
74	feeagh	raven	Edd feeagh vooar = nest of the great raven.
75	fo	under	Folieu = below the mountain.
76	foawr	giant	Meir y foawr = the giant's fingers (remains of a megalith on Lhergy Dhoo).

77	foillan	sea-gull	Lag ny voillan = hollow of the gulls.
78	freoagh	heather	Cronk froy = heather hill.
79	gaaue	smith	Boayl ny gaaue = place of the blacksmiths.
80	garee	shrubbery, waste land	Ballagarey = farm of the river shrubbery.
81	garey	garden	Garey keeill Vreeshey = garden of Bridget's church.
82	garroo	rough	Baare Garrow (Mx. *Bayr garroo*) = rough road.
83	geay	wind	Mwyllin ny geayee = windmill.
84	geinnagh	sand	Geinnagh Doo = black sand (strand).
85	giolcagh	broom	Cronk Guckley = broom hill; Ballajuckley = farm of the broom
86	glass	grey, green	Glaswoilley = green cattle fold.
87	goayr	goat	Glion ny Goayr = glen of the goats.
88	glion	glen	See No. 87, 46.
89	gob	point, promontory	Gob Liack = the headland of slates or flat stones.
90	gorrym	blue	Close Gorram = blue close.
91	guiy	goose	Curragh ne gey = marsh of the geese.
92	hoal	beyond	Garey Haul (Mx. *Garee hoal*) = further or outer garee (on Arragon).
93	howe	hill, headland	Ballnahowe = farm of the headland.
94	inneen	daughter, girl	Qoole Inyeene = girl's or daughter's nook.
95	irree	rising	Cronk yn Irree-Laa = hill of the dayrise (dawn).
96	jiarg	red	Broogh jiarg = red brow.
97	jiass	south	Yn magher jiass = the south field.
98	keeill	church	Lag ny Killey = hollow of the church. See also No. 81.
99	kerroo	quarter, quarterland	Kerrookeil = narrow quarterland.
100	keyl	narrow	Ballakeyll = small or narrow farm.
101	kione	head, end	Kione Droghad = bridge end; Kione ny Goggan = headland of the clefts or chasms.
102	laa	day	See No. 95.
103	lag, laggan, lig	hollow	Ballig = farm of the hollow. See also No. 77, 98.
104	lhean	broad	Slieau lhean = broad mountain.

A.	*Manx Gaelic*	*English*	*Examples*
105	lheannee	meadow	Cronk y Lheeannee= hill of the meadow.
106	lheeah	grey	Creg Lheeah = grey rock (in Glen Aldyn).
107	lhing	pool	Traie ny lhingey = shore of the pool. See also No. 114.
108	liargagh, lhergy	slope, hillside	Mwyllin ny liargee = mill of the slope; Lhergydoo = black slope.
109	liauyr	long	Fai lawr = long flat (on Ballaclague).
110	lieh	half	Lheakerroo = half quarterland.
111	logh	lake	Lough ny Baa = lake of the cow.
112	loghan	pond	Loghan y shuin = pond of the rushes.
113	losht	burnt	Cronk Lhost = burnt hill.
114	maarliagh	robber	Lhing y Vaarlee = the robber's pool.
115	magher	field	See No. 42, 97.
116	maynagh	monk	Ballamannagh = monks' farm.
117	mean, meanagh	middle	Ballameanagh = middle farm.
118	meayl	bald	Gob ny meayl = point of the bare or bald spot (Glen Aldyn).
119	moan, moanee	turf, turf-pit	Moanee mooar = big turfy field.
120	moddee	dog	Cronk y voddee = hill of the dog.
121	mollagh	rough, coarse	Mollagh vane = white rough place.
122	mooar, (vooar), moar	big	See Nos. 51, 74, 119.
123	mullagh	summit	Mullagh Ouyr = dun summit.
124	mwyllin	mill	See Nos. 83, 108.
125	noa	new	Ballanoa = new farm.
126	oaie	grave	Balla na haie = farm of the graves (by ancient cemetery). now Ballacraine
127	ooig	cave	Traie Ooigyn = shore of caves.
128	ouyr	dun	See No. 123.
129	pairk	enclosed pasture	Pairk y Chiarn = the Lord's pasture field.
130	ping	penny	Crott ne ping = croft of the penny.
131	poyll	pool	See No. 22.

132	purt	harbour	Purt ny Coan = narrow harbour; Ballafurt = harbour farm.
133	rea	smooth, flat	Traie rea = level strand.
134	reeast	moorland, waste	Rheast = waste or moorland.
135	rellick, rullick	cemetery	Faaie Rhullick = churchyard flat.
136	renniagh	fern	Bare na Ellan Renny (Mx. *Bayr yn ellan rhennee*) = road of the ferny isle (in Curragh district).
137	rheynn	division	Rentray (Mx. *Rheynn traie*) = shore division.
138	ruy	light red	Gob ruy = red naze or point.
139	sallagh	dirty	Chibbyrt poyll sallagh = well of the dirty pool (source of Glen Rushen river).
140	sallagh, shellagh	willow	Ballasalla = village of the sally or willow river (Gaelic name of Silverburn).
141	shenn	old	Shenn Valley = old farm.
142	shoggyl	rye	Cronk y shoggle = rye hill.
143	slieau	mountain	Kione slieau = mountain end.
144	slig	shell	Ballaslig = shell farm.
145	slogh	pit	Slogh, The = the pit.
146	stroean	stream	Strooan y kirkey = stream of the church.
147	tersyn	cross, crozier	Ballaterson = farm of the cross.
148	thalloo	earth, plot of ground	Thalloo noa = new land (newly enclosed mountain land).
149	thie	house	Thie Eary = shieling house.
150	towl	hole	Towl creg y vuggane = hole of the buggane's rock.
151	traie (tragh)	shore	See Nos. 70, 127.
152	trammon	elder tree	Glentrammon = glen of the elder or trammon trees.
153	twoaie	north	Yn magher twoaie = the north field.
154	ughtagh	hill	Ughtee crosh = hill of the cross.
155	unjin	ash tree	Glen Unjin = ash glen.
156	urley	eagle	Nock Urley = eagle's hill.
157	ushag	bird	Croit ny ushag = croft of the bird.

	A. *Manx Gaelic*	*English*	*Examples*
158	ushtey	water	Dul Ushtey = dark water (South of Niarbyl, from colour of seaweed on bottom).
	B. *Norse*		
159	a	river	Ramsey (Scand. *Ramsa*) = wild garlic river.
160	berg (berry)	rock, cliff	Farberry = firth or bay cliff (on coast between Laxey and the Dhoon).
161	byr (by)	homestead	Surby = moorland farm; Billown (*By* — *Lodinn*) = Lodinn's farm.
162	borg	small round hill	Burrow, Gaelicized form of *borg*.
163	dalr	dale, glen	Narradale = shieling dale (Scand. *Arg* or *Ergdalr*).
164	ey	island	Kella = cold isle (Scand. *Kaldey*).
165	eyland (ellan)	island	Giau yn Ellan = cave of the island.
166	fjall	fell, mountain	Snaefell = snow mountain.
167	fors (foss)	waterfall	Braid Foss = waterfall gorge.
168	gardr	garth, farm	Lhingague = an enclosure, small farm.
169	gata	road, gate	Raggatt = roe path or track.
170	gil	gill, ravine	Gilnas = ravine of the waterfall.
171	gja (giau)	creek, cave	Garwick (Scand. *Gjarvik*) = cave or *giau* creek.
172	Kirkja	kirk, church	Kirby = church farm; also see No. 146.
173	klettr (clet)	rock	Clett yn Stackey = rock of the stack (Calf).
174	nes	ness, headland	Langness = long headland.
175	sker	isolated rock	Skerestal = rock farm (Scand. *Skersstadr*).
176	stakkr (stack)	large rock	Cor Stack = round stack.
177	vik (wick)	creek	Dreswick = rock creek (Scand. *Drangsvik*: *Drangr*, is a lonely upstanding rock). See also No. 171.

(For full list see J. J. Kneen's 'Manx Place-Names' pp. 637-645)

INDEX